THIS IS
THE CARIBBEAN

THIS IS
THE CARIBBEAN

Text by Al Hornsby

Photographs by John Baker

NEW HOLLAND

First published in 1999 by
New Holland Publishers (UK) Ltd
London • Cape Town • Sydney • Auckland

24 Nutford Place
London W1H 6DQ, United Kingdom

80 McKenzie Street
Cape Town 8001, South Africa

14 Aquatic Drive
Frenchs Forest, NSW 2086, Australia

218 Lake Road
Northcote, Auckland, New Zealand

ISBN 1 85974 096 0

Designer: Daniël Jansen van Vuuren
Publishing Manager and Editor: Mariëlle Renssen
Cartography: Anton Krugel
Indexer: Annelene van der Merwe
Picture Researcher: Carmen Watts
Reproduction by Disc Express Cape (Pty) Ltd
Printed and bound in Singapore by
Tien Wah Press (Pte) Ltd

10 9 8 7 6 5 4 3 2 1

Illustrations appearing in the preliminary pages are as follows:
HALF TITLE: A Cuban woman, in the province of Santiago de Cuba.
TITLE PAGE: Spanish decorative elements on the Palacio Brunet, in
Trinidad, Cuba (left); a woman in rural Haiti (right).
THESE PAGES: Architectural detail from the Atlantis Paradise Island
hotel, Bahamas.
PAGES 6 and 7: The Queen Emma pontoon bridge spanning
St Anne's Bay in Curaçao's capital, Willemstad.

PHOTOGRAPHIC ACKNOWLEDGEMENTS

Ann Ronan Picture Library: 21; **Casement Collection**: 25, 40, 98 (top left), 99, 100, 102, 116 (top and bottom), 119, 123 (top), 135, 161 (top); **Christel Clear Picture Library**: 125 (top), 147 (top right); **Christel Clear Picture Library/Detlef Jens**: 15 (top right), 130 (bottom), 145 (top and bottom); **Colorific/Rob Crandall**: 34, 150, 151 (bottom); **Colour Library/Mike Hill**: 125 (bottom); **Al Hornsby**: 22, 59, 69 (bottom), 70 (bottom right), 71 (top), 72 (top left), 73 (top right), 91, 93 (top and bottom), 95 (left, right top and bottom), 96 (top right and bottom), 97, 156 (bottom left), 157 (bottom right), 163, 168 (bottom left and right), 169 (bottom right); **Hutchison Library/Robert Francis**: 147 (top left); **Hutchison Library/James Henderson**: 132 (bottom left); **Hutchison Library/Philip Wolmuth**: 46, 78 (top), 106 (left); **International Photobank/Adrian Baker**: 82 (top and bottom), 83; **International Photobank/Jeanetta Baker**: 12, 23, 33 (top), 41, 44, 47, 124 (top), 138; **International Photobank/Peter Baker**: 11, 14, 24, 26 (left), 31 (bottom), 32, 37, 39, 42, 45, 50, 51, 52, 53, 55, 62 (top right), 63 (bottom), 67 (right, top and bottom), 90, 98 (top right), 110 (top, bottom left and right), 111 (top and bottom), 112 (top and bottom), 113 (top and bottom), 115 (top and bottom), 118, 120 (bottom right), 121 (top, bottom left and right), 123 (bottom left and right), 124 (bottom left and right), 126 (top, bottom left and right), 127 (top and bottom left), 128 (top and bottom), 129 (top), 130 (top), 131 (top left and bottom left), 132 (top), 133 (right), 136, 137, 139 (top and bottom), 140 (top and bottom), 141 (top and bottom), 142 (top and bottom), 143 (top and bottom), 144 (bottom), 146, 147 (bottom), 151 (top), 161 (bottom); **International Photobank/Charlotte Rose**: 19, 172, 173 (bottom right); **Life File/Sean Finnigan**: 105 (top left and right); **Life File/Jeremy Hoare**: 8–9, 149; **Life File/Jason Holtom**: 144 (top); **Life File/David Kampfner**: 78 (bottom); **Life File/Richard Powers**: 76, 77; **Ocean Arts Inc/Bob Stearns**: 167 (bottom left); **Ocean Arts Inc/Walt Stearns**: 18, 57, 92 (top), 117 (top), 127 (bottom right), 148, 153 (top and bottom), 155 (top and bottom), 160, 166 (bottom), 167 (right), 168 (top); **Photo Access/G C Garner**: 10; **Photo Access/Don Hebert**: 122 (top); **Photo Access/R Sacha**: 27; **Photo Access/Arthur Tilley**: 131 (right); **Planet Earth Pictures/Pete Atkinson**: 108; **Planet Earth Pictures/I & V Durieux**: 129 (bottom); **Planet Earth Pictures/Ivor Edmunds**: 114 (top and bottom); **Planet Earth Pictures/Carol Farneti-Foster**: 169 (top left and right, bottom left); **Planet Earth Pictures/Doug Perrine**: 109 (bottom), 134; **Planet Earth Pictures/Margaret Welby**: 152; **Telegraph Colour Library/John Giustina**: 16; **Telegraph Colour Library/Geof du Feu**: 17 (bottom); **Mireille Vautier**: cover and spine, half title, full title (left and right), 20 (bottom), 26 (right), 79 (top and bottom), 80, 81 (top, bottom left and right), 84 (top and bottom), 85 (top and bottom), 86 (top and bottom), 87 (top and bottom), 88 (top left and right, bottom), 89 (top, bottom left and right), 103, 104, 105 (bottom), 107, 132 (bottom right), 133 (top left and bottom left), 162, 163 (top, bottom left and right), 165 (top, bottom left and right), 166 (top), 167 (top left), 171 (top right and bottom right), 173 (top and bottom left); **WaterHouse/Rick Frehse**: 70 (bottom left); **WaterHouse/Stephen Frink**: 13, 15 (bottom centre), 17 (top), 30, 49, 58, 63 (top), 64 (bottom), 70 (top), 96 (top left), 98 (bottom), 101 (top and bottom), 154, 156 (top), 159 (top and bottom), 170 (bottom); **WaterHouse/Bill Harrigan**: 15 (top left), 35, 72 (bottom left and right), 73 (bottom right), 75 (top and bottom), 92 (bottom), 94, 109 (top), 120 (top and bottom left), 122 (bottom right), 157 (bottom left), 171 (left); **WaterHouse/Darrel Jones**: 64 (top left); **WaterHouse/Robert Jureit**: 117 (bottom); **Lawson Wood**: 20 (top), 33 (bottom), 54, 62 (top left, and bottom), 67 (left bottom), 69 (top), 71 (bottom left and bottom right), 74 (left, right top and bottom), 122 (bottom left), 156 (bottom right), 157 (top), 158, 170 (top); **Hetty Zantman**: contents page (background), 28 (top and bottom), 29, 31 (top), 60, 61, 64 (top right), 65 (top and bottom), 66, 67 (left top and centre), 68 (top and bottom).

CONTENTS

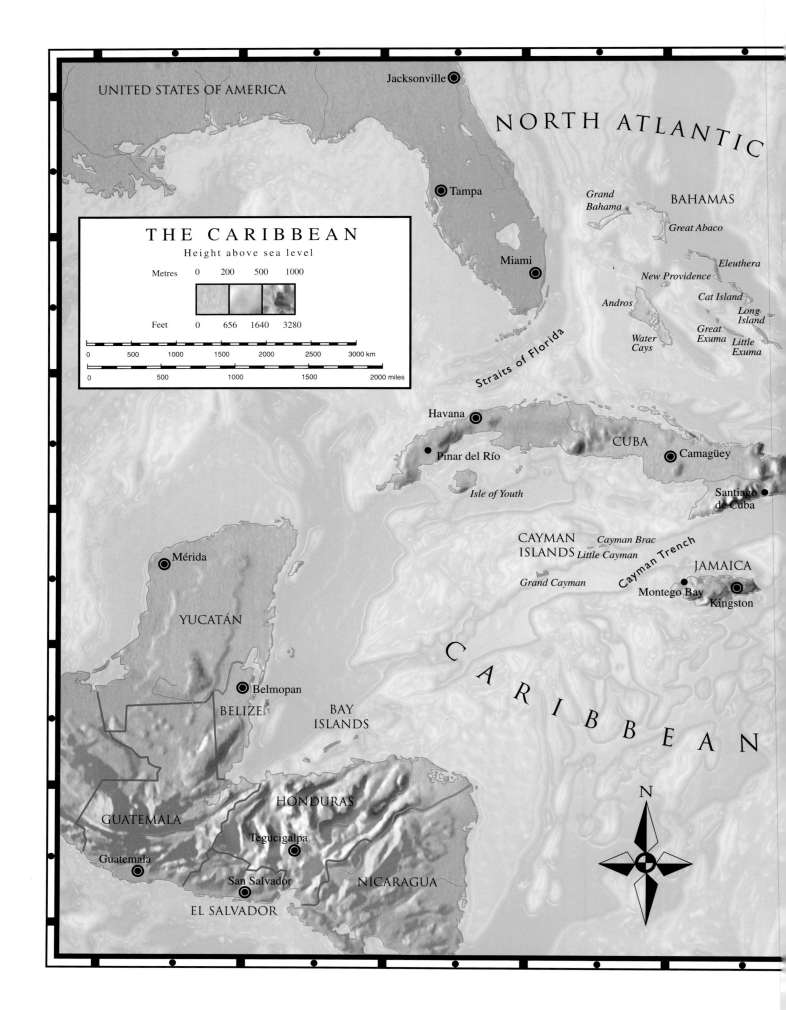

UNITED STATES OF AMERICA

Jacksonville

NORTH ATLANTIC

Tampa

BAHAMAS

Grand Bahama

Great Abaco

Miami

Eleuthera

New Providence

Cat Island

Andros

Long Island

Water Cays

Great Exuma

Little Exuma

THE CARIBBEAN

Height above sea level

Metres	0	200	500	1000

Feet	0	656	1640	3280

| 0 | 500 | 1000 | 1500 | 2000 | 2500 | 3000 km |

| 0 | 500 | 1000 | 1500 | 2000 miles |

Straits of Florida

Havana

CUBA

Pinar del Río

Camagüey

Isle of Youth

Santiago de Cuba

Mérida

CAYMAN ISLANDS

Cayman Brac

Little Cayman

Cayman Trench

JAMAICA

Grand Cayman

Montego Bay

Kingston

YUCATÁN

C A R I B B E A N

Belmopan

BAY ISLANDS

BELIZE

HONDURAS

GUATEMALA

Tegucigalpa

Guatemala

San Salvador

NICARAGUA

EL SALVADOR

N

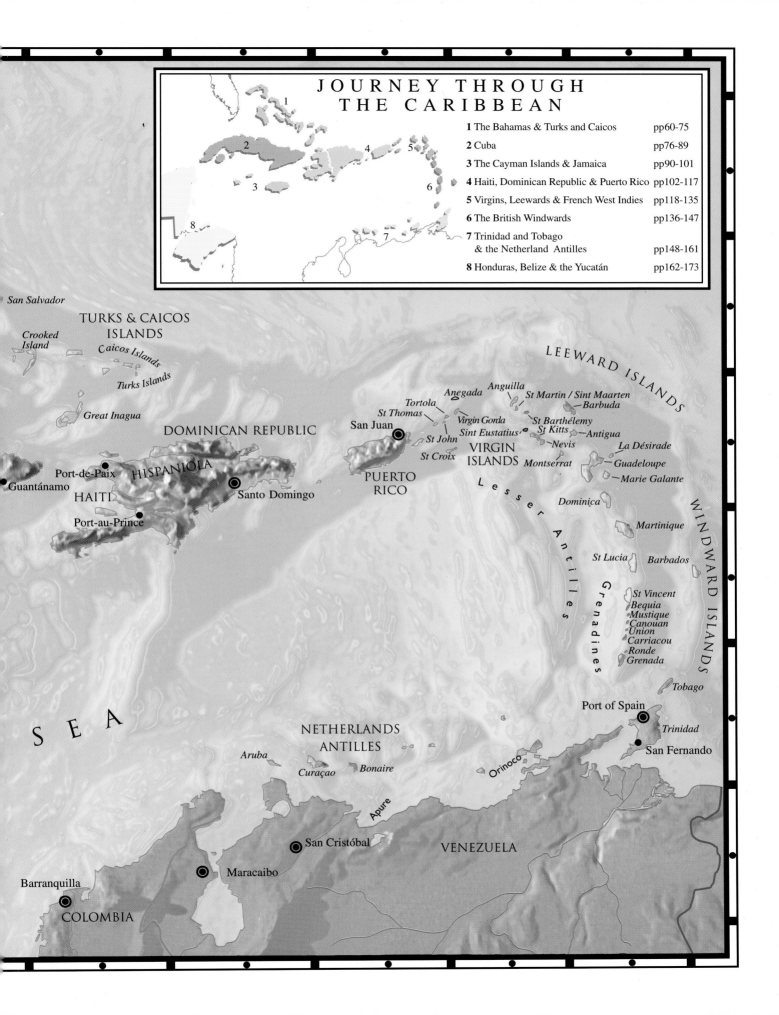

JOURNEY THROUGH THE CARIBBEAN

San Salvador

Crooked Island

TURKS & CAICOS ISLANDS

Caicos Islands

Turks Islands

Great Inagua

DOMINICAN REPUBLIC

HISPANIOLA

Port-de-Paix

Guantánamo

HAITI

Port-au-Prince

Santo Domingo

LEEWARD ISLANDS

Anegada   Anguilla

Tortola   St Martin / Sint Maarten

St Thomas   Barbuda

San Juan   Virgin Gorda   St Barthélemy

St John   Sint Eustatius   St Kitts

St Croix   Nevis   Antigua

VIRGIN ISLANDS   Montserrat   La Désirade

PUERTO RICO   Guadeloupe

Marie Galante

Lesser Antilles

Dominica

Martinique

St Lucia   Barbados

Grenadines

St Vincent

Bequia

Mustique

Canouan

Union

Carriacou

Ronde

Grenada

WINDWARD ISLANDS

Tobago

Port of Spain

Trinidad

San Fernando

SEA

NETHERLANDS ANTILLES

Aruba

Curaçao   Bonaire

Orinoco

Apure

VENEZUELA

San Cristóbal

Barranquilla

Maracaibo

COLOMBIA

PROFILE OF
THE CARIBBEAN

When you walk down a George Town street during Pirates' Week on Grand Cayman, part of the Cayman Islands which are cradled within the curve formed by Cuba to the north and Mexico's Yucatán Peninsula to the west, your senses are assaulted from every direction. The rhythms of reggae echo off the cobblestones; brightly dressed people – black, white, mulatto and mestizo – mingle, smiling faces and swaying movements replaying the music's happy message from within. Sharp, spicy food smells waft over the crowd: the sea-tinged smoke of broiling fish, the tang of jerk chicken, the bite of sizzling onions and peppers. Carts laden with mangoes, melons, bananas and limes throw splashes of colour along the congested avenues, and woven straw hats, baskets and mats spill richly from vendors' stalls. As you look around you, trying to take it all in, your vision widens to encompass quaint, colonial buildings of white stucco and grey stone. The duty-free treasures of Europe are displayed in countless small shop windows, collections of jewellery, fragrances, and designer fashion competing for your attention in every direction.

At the end of the bustling street, peacefulness reigns. Along the shore of the bay, coconut palms are silhouettes against a rich, sunset sky. The ocean, stretching away to the distant curved horizon, its bright turquoise now splashed with hues of pink and lemon, whispers over powder-sugar sand and coral as it softly swells and falls. The creak of sailboat rigging seems timeless, a reminder of ages past, when real pirates, heroes and villains of myth and legend, sailed these waters and walked these very shores.

And, as you gaze, you realize you have found the heart of it, you have suddenly understood a place, its style, its essence. For this – the throng of smiling, laughing, music-filled people; the underlying sense of colonial history and culture; the pervading presence of the warm, tropical sea – this, indeed, is the Caribbean.

AN INTRODUCTION

Images evoked by the Caribbean and its exquisite islands are long, deserted beaches, clear warm water and flowered jungle foliage. The Basin's cultures, though gently paced with unique touches of the exotic, nevertheless are familiar to European and American visitors.

This mix of impressions has made the Caribbean a tourist mecca, yet visitors quickly discover that there is no single description that fits the Caribbean as a whole. While there are commonalities of general lifestyle, the region is at the same time very diverse; the many islands and coastlines are geographically different, the climate varies, history differs, as do racial backgrounds. The complex interplay between a number of natural and historical forces, the various cultures that have been born of mixed traditions and those that have remained intact over the centuries all provide a fascinating study.

The region generally referred to as the Caribbean falls between latitude 10° north and the Tropic of Cancer, and its borders are Florida to the north, the Lesser Antilles to the east, Venezuela to the south, and Central America to the west. Of the region's hundreds of islands, some lie in the Caribbean Sea while others lie in the Atlantic Ocean. The term Caribbean, at times, is more cultural than geographic; indeed, listings of countries making up the area are seldom the same.

Navigator Christopher Columbus was perhaps the last to clearly identify the Caribbean when he termed the entire region the West Indies. It has been confusing ever since. Definitions sometimes exclude Central America and its islands, sometimes include Bermuda, far to the

PREVIOUS PAGES
Page 10: *Paradise Beach, Barbados.*
Page 11: *The brig* Unicorn *in Castries harbour, St Lucia, British Windwards.*

St Lucia's 'drive-in' Soufrière volcano (above), *so named for its accessibility to visitors, who can take their vehicles along a road leading directly into the crater itself.*

north off the USA, and at times include the Florida Keys. This is confused further when several groups of islands are referred to by both their geographical and political names.

The areas most often considered to make up the Caribbean would have the Bahamas and the Turks and Caicos as the northern boundary with the Greater Antilles forming the central portion. This is made up of Cuba, the Cayman Islands, Jamaica, Hispaniola (consisting of Haiti and the Dominican Republic), and Puerto Rico. The next group is the Lesser Antilles, a curved string of islands that marks the Caribbean Sea's border with the Atlantic, and comprises the Leeward Islands (the Virgin Islands, the French West Indies, the British Leewards and two of the Netherlands' islands) and the Windwards (the British Windwards, Barbados, and Trinidad and Tobago). The remainder, the southernmost islands of the Netherlands Antilles (also called the Dutch Leewards), lie off the Venezuelan

coast. To the west, where the Caribbean Sea meets Central America, are Honduras and its Bay Islands, Belize and its coral cays, and the Yucatán coast of Mexico, with its small island of Cozumel.

THE LAND AND SEA

The islands of the Caribbean Basin were formed by massive forces in a tectonically active area. The movement of the earth's crust along the Caribbean and American plates, where they intersect at the Puerto Rico Trench – running to the north of Puerto Rico and the US Virgin Islands in the Atlantic Ocean – has produced several different types of islands. Where material was thrust up from the deep ocean floor, mountainous islands like Cuba, Jamaica and Puerto Rico were formed. Where active volcanism occurred, especially along the Lesser Antilles chain, classic volcanic cone islands such as Guadeloupe, Martinique and St Vincent resulted. The area is still

'Mushroom Forest', in Curaçao's waters, is formed of mounds of boulder coral.

extremely volatile, and a number of the islands still have active volcanoes, boiling lakes, and geothermal hot springs. On Martinique, a huge eruption in 1902 destroyed the city of St Pierre; more recently, continual eruptions since 1995 of the Soufrière volcano on Montserrat, north of Martinique, have made much of the island uninhabitable.

In other areas, such as the Cayman Islands, crust movement raised steep-sided plateaus from the depths, and over the eons coral growth created islands atop them. Some islands, like the Bahamas, were formed not by tectonics but by corals growing along the edge of the North American continental shelf. The string of small islands along the coast of Belize in Central America are different: they are the only true coral atolls in the Caribbean.

Because of the nutrient-rich warm water, which ranges between 28 and 25°C (82°F and 77°F), coral growth is prolific throughout the Caribbean. All the islands and coasts have coral reefs to a varying extent and some landmass resulting from the industriousness of these small creatures. In areas of clearest water, especially around the drier islands and those without sediment-producing rivers, warm waters and sunlight penetrating deep into the sea are optimal for coral growth: islands such as the Bahamas, Turks and Caicos, the Cayman Islands, Cozumel, the Belizean atolls, Aruba, Curaçao and Bonaire are noted for their majestic coral formations.

And where there is coral there are also pure white sand beaches, made up of pulverized calcium carbonate, the substance from which corals are formed. It is no wonder that the Caribbean is famed for having some of the world's most beautiful glare-white sand beaches. Along the volcanic shorelines, there are black beaches as well, formed of jet-coloured, finely crushed lava sand.

CLIMATE

The entire Caribbean enjoys a tropical climate, with an average annual temperature of 25°C (77°F). While seasons are not significant, some variations do occur. For example, weather in the Bahamas, near the US mainland, can be influenced by the USA's winter storms, and temperatures may occasionally (though rarely) fall as low as 13°C (55°F).

Other areas are much less affected, and the average temperature range between the warmest and coldest months is only 3°C (5.5°F) for most of the Caribbean. Even in the highest mountain areas, some of which reach over 3050m (10,000ft), average temperatures are around 16°C (61°F).

Rainfall around the Caribbean region can differ markedly. In the Bahamas this ranges between 160mm (6in) of rainfall in the summer months (June, July and August) and 40mm (1.5in) in winter (January, February and March), which is similar to most of the Greater Antilles. In the southern Windward Islands, however, in places like Martinique and Trinidad, and along the Central American coastline, rainfall is more plentiful, with most months having at least 60mm (2in), and wet summer months having from 220–240mm (8.5–9in). Conversely, the southern Netherlands Antilles are extremely dry, with less than 20mm (0.5in) during the months of March, April and May, and usually not over 80mm (3in) in any month of the year.

Large rainfall differences can also occur on an island itself. Because the Caribbean Basin is in the path of the trade winds, which blow generally northeast to southwest, the windward sides of mountainous islands receive considerably more rain than the leeward sides. On many of the islands, high windward mountain slopes will be covered in lush rainforest, while nearby leeward slopes in the rain shadow may be very arid, with near-desert conditions.

Throughout the Caribbean, the most significant climatic changes are associated with the hurricane season, which is from mid-summer (July) through late autumn (November). The hurricanes are large, ocean-based cyclones that form in the Atlantic or southern Caribbean. Winds moving in a circular, clockwise direction develop around an area of extreme low pressure, known as the quiet 'eye'. These storms move westward and north, picking up strength over the warm Caribbean waters, and fierce winds and high rainfall can result.

An average of seven such storms a year move through the region, often with winds over 200kph (125mph), with occasional super storms having wind speeds in excess of 320kph (200mph). In recent years, the super storms Hugo, Gilbert and Mitch killed thousands of people and destroyed ships, towns and crops. Along with the high winds and waves, the rainfall resulting from such storms can cause widespread flooding and disastrous mud slides.

Fortunately for European and US tourists, the driest, most comfortable months in the Caribbean correspond to mid-winter in the north.

Poinsettia and trumpet vines are grown domestically and seen in the wild throughout much of the Caribbean.

FLORA

The Caribbean's climate provides a year-round growing season for a large variety of tropical vegetation. A number of different botanical environs occur throughout the Basin, generally the result of variation in the key factors: rainfall, altitude and soil-type.

The first common zone occurs at the sea, along the edge of iron shores or sand beaches. Similar to most tropical shores, this area is dominated by hardy, salt-tolerant plants and shrubs like Suriana and Beach Morning Glories. Coconut Palms grow in the shallow sandy soil, and *Scaevola* shrubs form a thick, low mat. *Lignum vitae*, with its intense blue flowers, and Seagrape grow further in from the high tide mark, and gnarled, thick-trunked West Indian Button trees grow at the sand's edge.

Inland on coral islands there are scrub pines, palmettos, and tough *Lepturas* grasses. *Lagenocarpus* sedges and scattered *Byrsonima* shrubs grow in sunny areas, and Cabbage Palms grow where the ground stays moist.

Along quiet bays, mangrove forests dominate, especially the Red Mangrove. This species (one of four) sends stilt-like roots into salt and brackish-water bottom layers, forming dense forests that protect shore areas from wave erosion and providing important habitat and breeding grounds for birds and many marine species. Freshwater marshes often border the mangroves, where many varieties of grasses, sedges and reeds flourish.

On the mountainous islands that receive ample rainfall, as well as along the Central American coast, tropical rainforest is common. These rich bio-zones are home to thousands of species of plants, animals and insects.

There are typically three major levels of vegetation, intertwined with lianas, vines and epiphytes (parasitic plants) – which include bromeliads, orchids and *Philodendrons*. The trees forming the top of the forest canopy (the dominants) can reach 46m (150ft) high, with mahogany species, the Crappo (or *Carapa guianensis*), Kapok, *Wild Chataigne*, Silk Cotton and Hog Plum as the main species. The middle level, or undercanopy, is populated by subdominants, which include *Bois Mulatre*, Cooperhoop, and Myrtaceae (myrtle) varieties. At ground level it is less dense, with ferns, small palms and *Helconia*. In areas where rainforests have been cleared, and on some larger islands like Cuba and Jamaica, large tropical grasslands occur, with tall grasses of several varieties, flowers and low shrubs.

HISTORY OF THE CARIBBEAN

For such a small area, the Caribbean has a remarkably complex history. While its recorded history began in 1492, after it was discovered by Italian navigator Christopher Columbus (whilst in the service of Spain), its ancient history began long before, with several different civilizations having developed in, or migrated through, the region. The earliest evidence of man along Caribbean shores, dating as far back as 10,000BC, existed in Mexico and other parts of Central America. Ice Age Man hunted there, following herds of woolly Mammoth and Musk Oxen down from the ice-bound north.

Agrarian societies began developing several thousand years later, and around 1000BC, the Olmecs, the first civilized culture to leave their mark on the land, appeared along the Central American Caribbean coast. The Olmecs worshipped fierce Jaguar-like gods who, according to their beliefs, demanded human sacrifice. The Olmec culture was considered to be a cruel one, despite the civilization's advances, which included the creation of writing and the New World's first calendar.

By 300AD, the Mayan Indian culture had emerged from the Olmecs' past. The Maya were an extremely accomplished people for their time, and their artistic and architectural achievements are still visible today, in deep jungle along the coasts of the Mexican Yucatán peninsula and Belize. They developed advanced astronomy and mathematics, but the power of this learning and education was tightly controlled by the priests and the small noble class.

By the year 900, a decline had begun and the rising militaristic Toltec culture exerted their influence. Less interested in the Maya's scientific and mathematical focus, they built a society based upon ceremony and community organization. In a very brief period of time, the advancements made by the Maya disap-

The Mayan temple at Uxmal, Mexico, is the most ornate in the Yucatán.

peared, lost in the ever-growing jungles. To this day, the reasons for the rapid Mayan decline remain a mystery. The Toltec's reign continued, apparently secure, until a fateful day in 1519 when, as was happening across the Caribbean Basin, a huge, many-sailed ship appeared, seemingly an apparition from the unknown. Captain Hernán Cortés of Spain had arrived, to put an end to the Toltec culture forever.

In other parts of the Caribbean, development had occurred much later and from different directions. Beginning sometime before the birth of Christ, Siboney Indians migrated south from Florida, occupying the Bahamas and the Greater Antilles. A peaceful people, they lived comfortably on the islands' bounty, hunting, fishing, and gathering a ready supply of naturally growing fruits, roots and vegetables.

At the start of the first century, another migration, the Arawaks from South America, began gradually absorbing the primitive Siboney culture as they moved northward, island by island. A more advanced people, their family-based

communal society fostered the development of plant cultivation, more efficient fishing techniques and boat building.

Living in groups of 500 and more, they established communities that benefited from division of labour among the sexes. The men cleared the land for agriculture, built boats, fished and hunted, while women's groups wove mats and baskets, made pottery and cultivated the crops. Their agricultural skills were surprisingly sophisticated, and they grew cassava, yams, maize, cotton, peanuts, spices and medicinal herbs. They also cultivated a plant that would later add to seafaring Europeans' intense interest in the area – tobacco.

While making no use of any written language, they did develop arts, some metallurgy, and were skilled woodworkers. Their health and success as a people also allowed them the leisure time to invent and participate in games, especially the ball game. Using a natural-rubber ball that could be struck with any part of the body except the hands, points were scored when the ball hit the ground on the opponent's side. Intense, organized competitions were held, and at times, games were used to settle disputes between rival communities.

Around 1000AD, another migration began northward out of South America, that of the warlike Caribs. A fierce people, they invaded and killed the peaceful Arawaks throughout the Lesser Antilles. They also made slaves of the vanquished tribes, forcing them into farm and domestic servitude. Demeaning their Arawak captives further, Carib men adopted a polygamous lifestyle, taking advantage of the large number of women available from the captured Arawak communities. While it has not been conclusively established, it is also believed that the Caribs became cannibals. Not only was the Caribbean named after this people, so too was the word for cannibal derived from them (the Arawakan words *caniba* and *carib* denote 'of Carib origin', while the Latin word *canibalis* means 'Carib').

Because of their fierce nature, they did not meekly accept the arrival of the Europeans as the Taino, a subgroup of the Arawaks, did in other parts of the region, and after early clashes they were subsequently avoided on some islands. While the entire Arawak race eventually died out of disease and deliberate slaughter (no full-blooded Arawaks remain), there are still some 2500 pure Caribs living in Dominica today.

Other than Mayan descendants in Central America, these few people, along with a small remnant of the Siboney Indians – the Lucayans of the Bahamas – are the only indigenous survivors left in the entire Caribbean. In the 500 years since Columbus first spotted his West Indian isles on the remote horizon, the world has virtually eradicated the region's bloodlines to its ancient past.

DISCOVERY AND COLONIZATION

Christopher Columbus walked ashore on the small island in the Bahamas now known as San Salvador on 12 October 1492 – and the race for riches and colonization had begun. By the 1530s, every country in Europe was embroiled in the struggle to capture the treasures and lands of the Caribbean. Following Columbus's four voyages for Spain between 1492 and 1504, during which he discovered and claimed the Bahamas, Cuba, Hispaniola (today Haiti and the Dominican Republic), Dominica, Guadeloupe, Trinidad, South America and the Central American coastline, other Spanish explorers – Hernán Cortés and Ponce de León among them – had established additional Spanish holdings in Florida, Mexico and Puerto Rico by 1521.

Invasions, sacks and conquests continued. Portugal followed with a small colony on Barbados in 1536, and for the next 250 years, warships representing all of Europe battled throughout the Basin. The Dutch took Cuba, Hispaniola, and Curaçao; the British took Puerto Rico, Barbados, Jamaica and Montserrat; the French moved onto Martinique

Ancient Arawak petroglyphs, like these on St Kitts, exist on many of the islands.

and St Kitts, and then took the western part of Hispaniola, calling it Haiti.

The conflicts and change of ownership of the lands in the region was exacerbated even further by the various wars, treaties and alliances in Europe during this period. Some islands changed hands

Statue of Christopher Columbus, Museo de la Ciudad, Havana, Cuba.

more than 20 times. To add to the chaos, the 30 years from the late 1600s until the 1720s has been called the Golden Age of Pirates, for good reason. Their plundering of ships and colonies created havoc throughout the Caribbean.

PIRATES OF THE CARIBBEAN

The region's pirates, real-life swashbucklers who sailed out of island strongholds to plunder shipping all the way from New England to South America, generated the most intriguing stories to come out of the history of the Caribbean. Flying various renditions of the skull and crossbones – also known as the 'Jolly Roger' – their fierce reputation for pillage, murder, and debauchery was well earned during the pirates' 30-year heyday.

Coming from many different backgrounds, the majority of the famous pirates were Englishmen; some began as simple seamen, others were ex-Navy and merchant fleet captains, and a few were even from the British upper classes. The early pirates were actually privateers who sailed with the blessing of the Crown: as long as they agreed to raid only ships owned by the hated Spanish, their activities were deemed acceptable.

THE CARIBBEAN ECONOMY

TOURISM

At one time valued mainly for its agricultural resources, the Caribbean has found an easier, more renewable and far more lucrative economic mainstay in modern times: tourism. In the beginning, the islands were chiefly a winter destination for nearby North America, but more recently the region has become a year-round vacation playground, and now attracts a global clientele.

Current estimates are that over 25 million people visit the Caribbean each year, with over five million of those from Europe. So important is this business to the Basin that for some island nations, tourism is the primary economic driving force. And, with the changing nature of the demands of world travellers, what is now being offered to them has been specially adapted to their needs. Vacationers are no longer satisfied to simply visit a place of beauty and lounge at the pool or the beach. Today's tourists are discerning in terms of the type of activities they seek. The nations of the Caribbean have responded dynamically, with a diversity of tourist opportunities.

The region's idyllic tropical ambience remains a powerful drawcard. To accentuate the experience, sumptuous upmarket hotels and resorts have been developed to offer pampered vacations. Antigua, Anguilla, Barbuda, and Barbados, particularly, have ultraluxury resorts while, on islands like Jamaica, some resorts are fashioned as self-contained enclaves where outdoor activities, sports, food and entertainment are included in the package price. This approach has been expanded to target different groups: singles, couples, families, and, especially, honeymooners. So lucrative is the honeymoon trade that many Caribbean countries have liberalized their marriage laws, making it easy for foreign visitors to hold their wedding ceremony as well as enjoy their honeymoon on some fantasy island hideaway.

Nassau's Paradise Island Hotel, a luxury tourist complex in the Bahamas.

Also associated with the resorts are casinos and golf courses, the former being especially popular in the Bahamas, Puerto Rico and the Netherlands Antilles. And while golfers the world over are familiar with the famous courses of Puerto Rico and Jamaica, excellent links courses have been established in most countries of the Basin.

In recent years, another form of luxury vacation has had a major economic impact on the region. Virtually every port in the Caribbean is now on the routes of large cruise ships carrying thousands of passengers, who can discover a number of different islands by making brief stops at each one. For sailing and motor yachting, the Caribbean may be the single most popular destination in the world. An abundance of anchorages throughout the islands are not only set in pristine surroundings, but encourage short cruises and ensure safety and comfort in protected waters. The Grenadines and the US and British Virgin Islands, ahead of all others, are centres for both charter and private boats. Each year, thousands of motorized and sail-ing craft manoeuvre in and out of the islands' serene anchorages.

To increase the Caribbean's appeal, attention is being directed to its beautiful natural resources, focusing on adventure and ecotourism, although no single activity has attracted more enthusiasts than diving. In the last 20 years, the region has become the world's most popular diving and snorkelling destination in terms of tourist figures. It is estimated that the US market alone spends over US$1 billion every year on Caribbean dive travel. For islands such as Cozumel and the Cayman Islands, diving has become the single largest tourist activity. Every nation in the Basin has clear, warm water, exquisite coral reefs and prolific marine life.

It is estimated that over 250,000 people try an introductory scuba diving experience each year in Caribbean waters. This is an activity that requires proper training and careful attention of safety measures. Fortunately for vacationers, the training necessary to enjoy a closely supervised dive with an instructor in shallow clear water takes only a few hours, and the Caribbean's close-to-shore reefs are ideal for such dives. At most of the region's tourist centres, professional dive operators provide Discover Scuba Diving or introductory programmes. Most resort areas have professional instructors licensed by PADI (Professional Association of Diving Instructors). Other instructional programmes available are NAUI (National Association of Underwater Instructors) and SSI (Scuba Schools International).

On the islands of the Lesser Antilles, visitors can hike to volcanoes, boiling lakes and through primeval rainforest. Rafting is popular in Jamaica, bird-watching in Trinidad and Tobago, whale-watching off the Dominican Republic, and cavern exploration in the Yucatán and Belize. And, for fishermen, few areas in the world are more highly regarded for big-game fish: Walker's Cay in the Bahamas has long been one of the world's best known spots, and Bimini, also in the Bahamas, was made famous by Ernest Hemingway, whose classic tale

The Old Man and the Sea was inspired by the area. Between the two islands, they are responsible for logging up nearly 50 game-fish records.

CONSERVING THE ENVIRONMENT

For the long-term future of its tourism, perhaps the most important issue facing the Caribbean is the protection of its environment. The nature of tourism creates a contradiction: well-preserved,

Drought-resistant plants, especially in the Agavaceae and Cacteae families, are typical of the arid islands.

pristine land and sea are necessary for the destination to be desirable, while the act of bringing in large numbers of visitors degrades the very environment that attracts them. The dredging of marinas and harbours and the building of beachfront resorts can cause silting that smothers coral reefs; packed resorts put

stresses on water resources and waste management systems; cruise ships can cause large-scale damage during anchoring and by offloading thousands of people into small communities whose roads, facilities and garbage-handling capabilities are scarcely adequate for the residents themselves.

As tourism's reliance on a healthy environment becomes increasingly clear, the governments of the Caribbean Basin are fortunately exhibiting far-sightedness and have made progress toward preservation. Led by scuba groups, many nations, especially the Cayman Islands, Cozumel, Belize, and Bonaire, have established marine parks that have been extremely successful in maintaining the quality of reefs and marine life, despite heavy use. Even where parks have not been formally established, bans on killing or harassing marine life and the taking of shells and other creatures have been broadly instituted and have been significant in protecting marine species.

On land, national parks and wildlife sanctuaries have been established in many of the Caribbean countries. Since many desirable tourist areas, especially the rainforests, are very sensitive to degradation, large uncontrolled numbers of visitors can cause lasting, if not permanent, damage. The establishment of such parks is crucial to the areas' survival. Properly managed, tourism may ultimately prove to be not only the Caribbean's most significant economic stimulus, but also its most powerful environmental benefactor.

SHOPPING

Shopping goes hand in hand with vacations and Caribbean merchants have learnt to appeal to every vacationer's whim. Local crafts, especially woven straw items, wood carvings, spices, peppers, and other packaged agricultural products are prolifically displayed, while huge quantities of imported goods are offered to visitors duty free.

In some destinations, like the Bahamas, Grand Cayman, the US Virgin

A straw market in the Bahamas.

Islands, St Martin, and Barbados, duty free shops seem to line the streets and arcades. Whether it's perfume from France, porcelain from England, cigars from Cuba, jewellery from South America or fashions from Italy, they are all available often at bargain prices.

Related to tourism is a substantial trade in condominium or vacation home ownership and time-share schemes. Many Caribbean nations have adjusted their laws to enable foreign investors to participate in local property ownership. When dwellings are not in use by the owners, they are rented to other visitors. The ongoing fees and taxes have become important sources of revenue for numerous small communities.

BANKING AND INSURANCE
In places like the Bahamas, the Cayman Islands (in particular), Jamaica and Tortola, visitors are often surprised at the large presence of banks. In the Cayman Islands alone the revenues generated are enormous; for a country with a population of only 36,000 people, there are 600 registered banks with assets in excess of US$500 billion. For the 28,000 foreign companies who do business with Cayman banks (similarly with other Caribbean banking areas), they enjoy the comfort of complete secrecy and no taxation.

The Cayman Islands and Tortola are also centres for offshore captive insurance companies. Established by foreign interests, these companies allow their owners to enter into the insurance business in the USA and Europe without the costs of high levels of capitalization and taxes, and also without the heavy regulation normally associated with the insurance industry.

AGRICULTURE
After tourism, the Caribbean's agriculture is its next most important economic resource. While not as significant as it was in colonial times, it remains integral to the overall economy. The Caribbean no longer holds the title Sugar Islands, but cane sugar is nevertheless an important export, with about one-quarter of the world's supply produced here. Once the main crop of most of the Basin's agricultural areas, sugar cane is a major crop today only in St Kitts, Guadeloupe and Barbados. On many islands, though, sugar cane is cultivated more specifically for the distilling of rum. Rum from well-known distilleries in Jamaica, Puerto Rico, Tortola, St Croix, Martinique, Barbados, and Grenada is shipped around the world.

In most areas, bananas have replaced sugar cane as the primary cash crop. Enormous banana plantations cover the landscape in farming regions. Other export crops include coffee, cacao, tobacco, nutmeg, ginger, and pepper, and various fruits such as mango, lime, pineapple, and papaya. For local consumption, small scattered farm plots yield a variety of vegetables and fruits such as maize, beans, pigeon peas, breadfruit, sweet potatoes, manioc (tapioca), taro, and avocados.

In rainforested areas, especially in Cuba, Trinidad and Central America, lumber is exported in significant quantities. Fine hardwoods such as mahogany and teak, as well as Caribbean Pine, are harvested both from natural forests and cultivated plantations. The availability of high-grade local woods also supports boat building, still a traditional craft in many areas throughout the Basin.

Still Barbados' chief crop, 60,000 tons of sugar cane are harvested annually.

islands the only topography, most of the rocky isles barely break sea level, their shorelines fringed with blinding white sand beaches – some 383km (238 miles) of beach in all.

The major islands are situated in two main groups, Grand Turk and Salt Cay in one, Pine Cay, Providenciales, and South, East, North and Middle Caicos in the other. The two groups are separated by the wide Turks Islands Channel. Because of the lack of habitation, the area has much wilderness, with 33 different established preserves and parks. Salt ponds and marshes are scattered throughout, with thick mangroves in some bays. The arid climate supports mainly scrub, thorny acacia species and cacti. Trees are scarce, having been removed to aid salt production during colonial times.

Wildlife thrives in the preserves, with little pressure from any encroaching development. Like in many island environments, birds are the most numerous terrestrial animals. There are many sea and wading birds, including frigates, pelicans, tropicbirds, stilts, plovers and flamingos. Surprising numbers of raptors are also present, among these, ospreys, harriers, Peregrine Falcons and Red-tailed Hawks.

Mammals are not numerous, except for a few wild cattle and two species of bat, but there are some interesting reptiles, such as iguanas and an endemic snake, the Pygmy Boa. Marine life, on the other hand, is rich and prolific. Because the islands rise up directly from deep water, many pelagic species are seen near to shore. There are tuna, jacks, Eagle Rays, and Loggerhead Turtles. Humpback Whales migrate through on their way to calving grounds at the nearby Silver Banks.

For scuba divers, the reefs drop away in steep, majestic underwater walls that are covered with sponges, corals and sea fans. With its crystal-clear water, the Turks and Caicos islands offer some of the most pristine and spectacular diving in the entire Caribbean Basin.

The first permanent settlements of Bermudian salt-rakers in the 1700s found little trace (except for some old dwelling sites that still can be seen) of the original Arawak Indian inhabitants; all had died within 50 years of having been discovered by Europeans (either Columbus or Ponce de León; historical records are unclear). During the American Revolution in the 1770s, the Bermudians were joined by British loyalists from the USA, needing a safe haven. They brought in African slaves and started cotton plantations, which eventually failed. Other immigrants were smugglers and pirates, who found that the remote, desolate location suited their needs.

Today, the 14,630 residents are either black, mulatto or expatriate. The islands, after having been a part of both the Bahamas and Jamaica at various times during their past, are now a British dependent territory. The Queen of England is represented locally by her appointed governor, who appoints both the chief minister, the head of the local government, and six of the seats of the Legislative Council; the remaining 13 seats are elected.

With some export revenues from Spiny Lobster, and conch flesh and shells, the islands are very dependent upon tourism; 70 per cent of the 85,000 tourists each year arrive from the USA. A number of resorts and hotels serve visitors, who come chiefly for scuba diving and other watersports, sunbathing and bird-watching. The idyllic islands certainly offer more of an 'off-the-beaten-track' experience.

CUBA

Cuba, at over 110,860km^2 (42,850 sq miles) the largest island in the Greater Antilles and the Caribbean, is most known for being the only communist country in the region.

The island is lovely, with rolling grasslands, mountains that reach 2005m (6578ft) and a varied, undeveloped coastline of rocky cliffs and white sand beaches bordered by the sea. National parks protect a variety of plant and animal life, with forests of mahogany and Caribbean Pine, Flame and coral trees. Flowers of great variety include the Butterfly Bush, Cuba's national flower,

Fidel Castro, leader of Cuba, the only communist nation in the Caribbean. He has remained firmly in power since his successful revolution in 1959.

Verbena and the Trumpet Plant. Several rare, endemic animal species feature on the 'world's smallest' list: the Bee Hummingbird, the Pygmy Frog, and the Almiqui, a shrew-like insect eater that is the smallest mammal ever discovered.

Like most Caribbean nations, Cuba's present is still directly tied to its colonial past. Discovered by Columbus on his first voyage in 1492, the island was developed by Spain for agriculture, mainly sugar and tobacco. Slaves were imported from Africa as early as 1526 and were used until nearly 1890, unlike other areas in the basin where slavery ended in the early 1800s. Some 435,000 slaves worked the plantations. This resulted in a strong, ingrained conflict with landowners, and slave revolts occurred regularly throughout the 19th century. Even today, this late-era slavery has left its cultural mark. African traditions were kept intact much later than in most of the Caribbean and still have a strong influence on food, art, music and dance. The make-up of the population of 11 million reflects this history too: 51 per cent are mulatto, 37 per cent white Hispanic, 11 per cent black, and the remainder are Chinese.

Cuba came under US ownership when the USA sided with rebels in a revolution against the Spanish in the 1890s. The sinking of the battleship USS *Maine* in Havana harbour brought the USA into a brief war with Spain; Cuba was ceded as a result. The USA soon granted independence in 1902, and a series of dictatorial governments ruled, without conceding to the populace's demand for land reform. This gave rise to Fidel Castro's communist revolution, and he took power in 1959. The result is one of the more interesting political conflicts in modern times; the former US territory, which sits just 147km (90 miles) off the American coast and still has a US naval base (Guantánamo), is the only communist country in the region, one much at odds with the USA. Cuba's government, with Castro in place as president of both the Council of State and Council of Min-

isters, as well as the head of the Communist Party, is still intact. However, with the loss of Soviet financial support, Cuba has begun developing trade and tourism to a level far beyond what existed in the past.

Besides sugar and tobacco – historically Cuba's most important exports, but both were severely damaged by Hurricane Lili in 1996 – exports are nickel, medicinal products, coffee, and shellfish.

Tourism has now surpassed sugar as a revenue producer, and visitors find Cuba a fascinating place in which to vacation. During the first half of the 20th century, Havana gained fame for its music, dance, casinos and resorts, an inspiration perhaps for the new resorts that are beginning to open, with tourist services being upgraded although progress is slow: antiquated buildings and vehicles are the norm. Churches, forts, statues, and antiquities on display in architecturally elaborate museums provide a strong visual representation of Cuba's long history, and exhibit colonial Spanish and post-revolution influences. Windows with brightly painted wood or metal frames, wrought-iron grilles and

decorated balconies are some of the ubiquitous Cuban ornamental details.

Scuba diving is becoming an increasingly popular attraction, as Cuba's reefs are largely pristine and there has been very little commercial fishing to affect marine life over the years. The result is that reefs are vibrant and alive with schools of tropical fish. The waters around the Isla de la Juventud, perhaps the most popular diving area, have been declared a marine park.

THE CAYMAN ISLANDS

Lying south of Cuba and northwest of Jamaica, the Cayman Islands are low coral and limestone islands that sit alone in the cobalt-blue Caribbean Sea. Grand Cayman, with its capital city George Town, is the largest, while Little Cayman and Cayman Brac lie near each other to the northeast. The islands are noted for their warm clear waters and remarkable white beaches. In fact, Grand Cayman's Seven Mile Beach is regarded as one of the most beautiful in the entire Caribbean. Despite no sources of fresh

The popular wreck dive, Oro Verde, *off Grand Cayman. The Cayman Islands are considered to be one of the world's top diving destinations.*

water, the tropical climate keeps the islands green, with vegetation typical of coral islands. Coconut Palms dot the shoreline here and there, and Seagrape lines the beaches, with pines further inland. Large expanses of mangrove forest surround the islands' substantial lagoons, and there are flowers in profusion, among them domesticated flowering shrubs such as hibiscus, oleander and bougainvillea. The *Oncidium calochilum* and *Schomburgkia thomsoniana* species are two of three rare endemic orchids that occur here.

Again, local animal life is limited except for birds, although native species have been significant in the Caymans' history. Originally named Los Tortugas by Columbus for the many turtles he found nesting there, the name that has lasted derives from another local reptile, though now extinct: *caymanas* in the Carib language means 'small crocodile'. Because of a very successful replenishment programme carried out by the Cayman Turtle Farm, Green Turtles are again plentiful. Other reptiles include iguanas, Cayman Anoles, and two non-poisonous snakes.

Mammals are few, and include the Cayman Rabbit, a few Agouti (a member of the rodent family), and several species of bat. Birds are prolific, with over 200 species, and sanctuaries on all the islands provide nesting sites for Cayman Parrots, Red-footed Boobies, frigates, Smooth-billed Anis, West Indian Whistling Ducks, herons and many other wading birds, which flourish in the shallow lagoons.

The waters around the Cayman Islands are especially rich with life, and in combination with the calm clear conditions, have made the islands the Caribbean's top-ranked diving destination. There are groupers, snappers, jacks, large Tarpon and Eagle Rays around the beautiful coral reefs and dramatic undersea walls. Schools of brightly coloured tropical fish – angelfish, butterflyfish, parrotfish and many more – are practically everywhere, including around

the Caymans' famous shipwrecks, the *Balboa*, the *Oro Verde*, and the Russian destroyer MV *Captain Keith Tibbets*.

Perhaps most well-known of the Cayman Islands' dive attractions, however, is a school of nearly 200 friendly Southern Stingrays that gathers around excited snorkellers and divers to be hand-fed at a site known as Stingray City off Grand Cayman.

Discovered accidentally by Columbus on his fourth voyage in 1503, the islands were first settled in the 1600s by escaped slaves and British army deserters from Jamaica. A French fleet with 500 slaves, escaping from the Dutch, joined them in 1677, and additional settlers came from England and Scotland on a royal land grant in 1734. Pirates and privateers also frequented the islands during the American Revolution, as the then uninhabited isles of Cayman Brac and Little Cayman provided perfect hideaways.

The Caymans were a dependency of Jamaica until the latter became independent in 1962. They decided thereafter upon British dependent territory status, which they maintain todày. Administered by the Queen's appointed governor, local representation isaccomplished through a Legislative Assembly, with 15 of the 18 seats elected, the other three seats being appointed by the governor. Advising the governor is an Executive Council, with three members appointed by the governor and four elected by the Legislative Assembly.

The islands' 36,000 people, all but a few thousand of whom live on Grand Cayman, are 40 per cent mixed race, 20 per cent black, 20 per cent white, and 20 per cent expatriate. They enjoy a comfortable lifestyle, with one of the highest living standards in the world: the average Caymanian's annual income is US$68,000.

Despite the healthy tourism industry – a million visitors a year come for diving and other watersports, and to enjoy the sun at the Caymans' many upscale resorts – the real underpinning of the

economy is the unique position the islands hold for offshore financial services. Some 600 registered banks have made the Cayman Islands the world's fifth largest financial centre, and the resulting revenues account for 70 per cent of the islands' Gross National Product (GNP).

JAMAICA

When Columbus discovered Jamaica in 1494, he must have realized that he had found one of the most beautiful islands in the New World. The Arawaks living there when he arrived had named it for its ample waters (*chaymaka* means 'well watered'), emerging from a profusion of springs, rivers and waterfalls. With rainforest-covered mountains reaching 2256m (7402ft), a high grassy plateau and a coastline interspersed with sand beaches and mangrove-filled bays, the 245km-long (150-mile) island clearly was a valuable find.

The waterfalls of the interior are appealing, as are the meandering, slow-moving rivers for their bamboo-raft cruises. Tracts of primeval rainforest still exist in several areas, and the dense woodlands comprise mahogany, Balsa and many species of palm. There are several thousand different flowering plants, and in one unique area named 'The Gully', over 300 varieties of ferns – Holly, Maidenhair, Brake, Sword and Rabbit's Foot, among others – grow in the lush jungle. The rainforest is home to many birds, 25 species of which occur nowhere else. Endemics include the Jamaican Tody, Yellow-billed Parrot, and the hummingbird species Doctorbird, which is the island's national bird. A few reptiles are seen, such as the American Crocodile and Jamaican Iguana, and the small Hutia is one of the relatively few indigenous mammals. Mongooses, originally introduced to kill rats, are prolific, and in the shallow bays are two marine mammals: the Manatee and Pedro Seal.

When the first Spanish colony was established in 1509, the settlers planted

Ocho Rios is a regular port of call in Jamaica for luxury cruise liners. Cruise ships stop at virtually every island in the Caribbean, bringing hundreds of thousands of tourists each year for sightseeing, shopping and watersports.

cacao and coffee, and the Arawaks were quickly exterminated. When slaves were introduced from Africa in 1517, Jamaica's economic importance was quickly established, with sugar production becoming the leading activity. The British eventually took the island from Spain in 1655 and added indigo, cotton and tobacco to its plantation lands. Jamaica soon became Britain's most valuable Caribbean colony.

After the abolishment of slavery, sugar, similarly with other islands in the region, lost its economic importance as an export, and most of the 600 sugar

mills deteriorated into ruins. Sugar cane was still grown, but in smaller quantities, chiefly for rum production. Bananas ultimately became the most important export crop.

Jamaica eventually became independent in 1962, remaining an independent state within the Commonwealth. The Queen of England is still recognized as the chief of state, represented by her governor general, who appoints the prime minister. He also appoints the members of one of the legislative bodies, the Senate, with the House of Representatives being elected by the

populace. Jamaica's 2,615,000 people – 77 per cent black, 13 per cent mulatto, 3 per cent white, and the balance mainly East Indian (from India) and Chinese – speak English and local Creole.

Today, the economy is healthy, with the current government having instituted perhaps the most progressive economic reforms in the region. Bauxite and refined alumina generate nearly 50 per cent of export revenues, with tourism the next most important industry. With nearly a million visitors a year, Jamaica is the fourth largest tourist destination in the Caribbean. Tourists stay predominantly on the north coast, with less than a quarter of them visiting Kingston, the capital, where a high population has resulted. Unfortunately, the crime rate is also high. The north coastal region has become known for its luxury all-inclusive resorts, which offer guests virtually everything from golf and watersports to entertainment on the property, and all included in the cost of staying here.

Of all Jamaica's attractions, however, its most memorable is likely to be its music. Reggae, now one of the world's most popular music forms, is a combination of the African-derived style of *mento* and 1930s American rhythm and blues. Its characteristic sound is its emphasis on the usually unstressed beats of a musical bar. The reggae culture is greatly influenced by another of Jamaica's most recognizable icons – dreadlocked Rastafarians. The Rastas are religious followers of the belief that Africans are the chosen race; their practice is to follow Nature's way, in hairstyle, dress and their ritualistic smoking of ganja (or marijuana), a herb long used in Jamaican folk medicine.

HAITI

Just east of Cuba, occupying roughly one-third of the island of Hispaniola, is the mountainous nation of Haiti. Although it is the poorest, least developed country in the western hemisphere, the unspoiled land that remains is, indeed, lovely, with virgin montane cloud forest atop the Massif de la Selle mountain range. The forests are still home to 140 species of orchid and an entire ecosystem composed of ferns, mosses and liverworts.

Small reptiles, bats (Fruit and Brown Flower species), butterflies, amphibians, and birds – all reclusive species of the mist – move through the quiet mountain terrain. Lake Saumatre is still the haunt of the American Crocodile, and flocks of Greater Flamingos and other waterfowl.

The countryside is dotted with many ruined forts and plantations from colo-

nial days. In a handful of museums, remarkable collections of local paintings, wood carvings and intricate woven articles are on display. Haitian art, music and dance, which form an integral part of their chief religion, voodoo – a combination of West African spirit worship and tenets borrowed from Roman Catholicism – infuse the very fabric of their society; at one time the arts were considered among the most well-developed in the entire Caribbean.

Local cuisine, generally highly regarded for its quality and flavours, is a spicy combination of French and Creole.

First colonized by France in the 1600s, Haiti was considered at one time to be the most valuable of all the Caribbean colonies. However, its first slave revolt in 1791 was merely the beginning of a conflict, inspired by racial hatred and repression, that would continue into modern times. After independence from France was achieved in 1804, the Haitian people turned their racially directed aggression on each other: the black population – 95 per cent of the total and descended directly from African slaves – and the mulattos – descended from slaves and French owners, have continuously struggled against each other for power ever since.

Throughout the revolutions and coups of the last two centuries, the agricultural infrastructure, once so well-developed, gradually disappeared and the deforested, untended land eroded away. The population, fuelled by poverty and lack of education, has continued to grow unchecked. Finally, however, mounting internal strife, atrocities and continual election fraud in the 1980s and 1990s brought intervention by the United Nations, and Haiti experienced its first peaceful transition of a freely elected government in 1995.

Even so, a general lack of law enforcement, little foreign investment and an overall absence of opportunity have left a poor, struggling society. One direct result has been the 'boat people' exodus where, since the mid-1980s, hundreds

of thousands of Haitians attempted desperate, dangerous escapes to other countries. Seventy-five per cent of Haiti's 6.6 million people live in abject poverty, the literacy rate is only 45 per cent, and 70 per cent of the economy is dependent on agriculture, on land that is extremely damaged. Haiti's future therefore remains difficult.

With an elected president and his appointed prime minister, and an elected legislature, the National Assembly, now in place, the hope exists that there is at least the basis for new beginnings, although any progress will be slow. The 27 different political parties will undoubtedly make it difficult to push major plans quickly through the governmental process. There is also little hope for the redevelopment of tourism in the near future; crime is too high and infrastructure too weak.

THE DOMINICAN REPUBLIC

Covering the eastern two-thirds of Hispaniola, the Dominican Republic is one of the more unique nations of the Caribbean. Despite a chaotic and often traumatic past, the country retains a remarkable natural beauty, with extensive areas of pristine deserted beaches and also the highest mountains – part of the Cordillera Central – in the Basin. The highest peak, Pico Duarte, rises to 3175m (10,417ft). In the mountains, stands of Caribbean Pine cover high slopes, and large areas of virgin rainforest harbour orchids, *Philodendron*, palms and mahogany trees.

Cotica Parrots (the national bird), Guaragua Hawks, Great Hummingbirds and many other species make the area a popular bird-watchers' destination. In arid parts of the country, there are parks preserving wild lands covered with acacia and 10 different varieties of cactus, and supporting endemic birds like the Querebebe and the Cu-cu, and wildlife such as the Hutia and iguana species. In the coastal regions, there are parks with

cent of whom are descended from black slaves, enjoy a tranquil existence and are welcoming and friendly.

At the extreme northeast end of the chain the island, **Anegada**, is a flat coral cay surrounded by a huge protected coral reef that teems with marine life. The reefs are also the resting place for a multitude of ships that went down over centuries of sailing. On shore, wild donkeys and goats, and herons, ospreys, flamingos and terns thrive, the birds finding nesting areas in the mangroves around the isle's large lagoon. On Anegada's longest beach, 18km (11 miles) of talcum-powder sand, people are the scarcest commodity. At certain times of the year, the crowds consist of Hawksbill, Green and Leatherback Turtles coming ashore at night to lay their eggs.

Discovered by Columbus in 1493, the British Virgins were initially settled by the Dutch, then taken by the British in 1666. When the West Indian Federation was formed in 1958, the locals decided not to join in a move toward independence, but instead remained a British dependent territory. Today, the Virgin Islands' 14,000 residents, over one-half of whom live on Tortola with most of the remaining population on Virgin Gorda, are administered by the Queen's governor and the governor's local appointee, here called the chief minister. An elected Legislative Council provides input from the populace.

The economy is extremely dependent upon tourism, especially from sailing, yachting and diving, which accounts for 45 per cent of revenues. With quiet, protected anchorages scattered throughout the islands, the British Virgins are ideal for boating. For scuba divers, not only are the local waters clear, warm and full of marine life, they are also home to one of the most celebrated shipwrecks, the royal mail carrier *The Rhone*, which went down in a hurricane in 1867. Today, it is a fascinating and beautiful dive region enjoyed by enthusiasts from around the world. The islands also feature many upmarket resorts, tucked away in lush

remote locations that successfully maintain the peaceful local flavour.

Besides tourism, rum and fresh fish are exported, though not in large quantities. An important new industry has been growing in recent years – that of international business and mutual fund corporate registration. Carefully maintained secrecy laws, low corporate registration fees and substantial tax advantages have led to over 210,000 companies registering in the British Virgin Islands in recent years. Mutual funds represented in the islands are currently worth well over US$5 billion.

THE BRITISH LEEWARDS

The British Leewards are the past and present British colonies of the Leeward chain. Anguilla is the furthest north, located just east of the British Virgin Islands, and the rest – St Kitts and Nevis, Antigua and Barbuda, and Montserrat – lie curved to the south–southeast, between Anguilla and the French island of Guadeloupe. The various islands are either volcanic or low limestone isles, and despite a few individual differences, share a similar history. Except for Anguilla, whose discovery – whether by the French in 1564 or the Spanish sometime earlier – is debated, all of the British Leewards were discovered by Columbus on his second voyage, in 1493. Interested particularly in gold and silver on that trip, he noted the small islands but passed them by, looking for larger lands more likely to have substantial mineral deposits. That the islands were all inhabited by fierce Carib Indians, who had themselves taken the isles from the Arawaks some 400 years earlier, undoubtedly further lessened his interest.

The islands were settled by the British, beginning in the early 1600s, and after various periods of conflict with the indigenous Caribs (who were all ultimately destroyed within the next 50 years) and the French, the UK finally

took full control, aided by the strength of its fleet based in Antigua. The islands eventually became independent nations within the Commonwealth or have remained British colonies.

Noted for their great natural beauty and colonial charm, and as a result the tourism that has become such an important factor to their economies, the islands have been significantly affected by hurricanes in recent years. Hurricane Hugo, in 1989, destroyed much of Montserrat, damaging 95 per cent of its housing, and caused significant destruction to Nevis, though the island was well-prepared and recovered swiftly. Antigua and Anguilla were hit hard by Hurricane Luis in 1995, and their water, power and tourist infrastructures were severely damaged. Fortunately, repairs were begun quickly, and the British Leewards have regained much of their popularity.

ANGUILLA

Anguilla is a small flat coral island, just 91km² (35 sq miles) in size, green with low scrub that's tolerant of hot sun and periods of little rain. With no run-off and little development, its surrounding waters are sparkling clear, turquoise along the shore and cobalt blue in the depths. With its scattering of small islands and long deserted stretches of pure white sand – some 18km (12 miles) in all – it is a sun-worshipper's dream. Its quiet 'South Seas' ambience has made it a favourite with American visitors, who make up 65 per cent of its arrivals, upscale tourism being the major economic activity.

Bird-watchers frequent its Little Bay area, where 93 species of birds occur, including Blue-faced Boobies, Great Herons and kingfishers.

The island is also enjoyed for its scuba diving and snorkelling. A great number of shallow coral reefs teeming with schools of brilliantly coloured fish fringe the island's shores, and there are a number of shipwrecks – nine of them have been sunk recently, specifically for the enjoyment of divers.

The 10,785 residents, mainly black and mulatto descended from African slaves and the original English and Irish settlers, have maintained their status as a dependent territory of the UK. The Queen's appointed governor and his appointed chief minister head the government, along with a legislative body, the House of Assembly of which seven of the members are elected, the other four appointed by the governor. Anguilla, at one time joined with St Kitts and Nevis, opposed the union and after civil strife in the 1970s, the island was declared a separate colony in 1980.

With its centre of government and commerce – and the highest population – in the town of The Valley, the nation's economy, besides tourism, is fuelled by lobster and salt exports, and revenues from offshore banking. Similarly with other islands of the Leeward and Windward chains, Anguilla's banking secrecy laws and proximity to the South American drug trade have brought questions of money-laundering at various times, with accompanying political scandals.

ANTIGUA AND BARBUDA

Antigua and Barbuda, after their original French and Spanish settlements failed because of Carib hostility, were established by the British and remained crown colonies until independence was reached in 1981. Antigua, with a well-fortified naval base in its harbour, was the centre of British colonial rule for the entire Caribbean. Its capital, St John's, is still very attractive, with many examples of restored colonial architecture.

This two-island nation, with a present population of 64,000 people – all but two per cent of African slave descent – is now a self-governing, parliamentary democracy, following the British structure. The Queen is still recognized, and is represented by her appointed governor general, as chief of state. The nation's head of government is the appointed prime minister, who works with a Parliament. The Senate is appointed by the governor general, while

A Papaya tree bears fruit above Dickenson Bay, Antigua.

the House of Representatives is elected by proportional representation.

Because of the difficult times faced by the islands' slaves after their emancipation in 1834, political strife founded on racial themes of differential empowerment and opportunity has been common even in modern times, with turmoil as recent as the early 1990s.

Antigua, the more developed of the two islands, has rolling volcanic hills in the west with its highest point, Boggy Peak, attaining a height of 402m (1319ft), and a low flat plain of limestone stretching eastward. Denuded of trees in the late 1600s by plantation owners for sugar cane cultivation, the island is now rather dry, but has enough rainfall to support low greenery and a number of different flowering trees. With palm-lined beaches and graceful coves along its shoreline, it is picturesque and restful. For nature-lovers, the area around McKinney Salt Pond is noted for its many birds, some 150 species in all. Enormous flocks of sandpipers wade

through the shallows, and there are nesting areas for the unusual Yellow-crowned Night Heron. On Great Bird Island are Red-billed Tropicbirds, and during the summer and autumn months, Hawksbill Turtles lay their eggs on quiet beaches.

The economy is largely dependent on tourism, with some light manufacturing being developed. Its sugar-cane-based agriculture disappeared within 12 years of the worldwide drop in sugar prices in 1960. Today, farming focuses on locally consumed crops of fruits, vegetables and coconuts.

Barbuda, which sits 40km (25 miles) north of Antigua, is a coral isle formed around a large lagoon and has only 1000 residents. It is noted for its beautiful beaches, and there are more than 100 shipwrecks around its many reefs, attracting scuba divers. Watersport operators are based in the chief town of Codrington, named after the family who once owned the island.

When not diving and snorkelling, visitors also enjoy Barbuda's wildlife, which is more prolific than on most other islands of the area. Ducks, guineafowl, plovers, and pigeons can be seen, as well as deer, wild pigs, horses and donkeys – escapees from settlements in colonial times.

ST KITTS AND NEVIS

The two-island constitutional monarchy of St Kitts (formally St Christopher, as named by Columbus) and Nevis are dramatic, green volcanic islands located due west of Antigua.

St Kitts has several peaks, the highest being Mount Liamuiga (previously known as Mount Misery), at 1156m (3793ft). Liamuiga is derived from the Carib word for 'fertile land'. Nevis is a single cone, Nevis Peak, which rises to 985m (3232ft). The two islands are actually a continuous land mass; the ridge connecting them lies just 8m (25ft) beneath the surface of the 3km-wide (2-mile) channel that separates their shores.

The islands are breathtakingly beautiful, with high mountains rising dram-

Frigate Bay at St Kitts, with Nevis visible in the distance. The volcanic islands have lush mist- and rainforest on their higher elevations, and panoramic views.

familiar colonial pattern. After being discovered by Columbus, they were settled in 1623 by the British. The French took over a portion of St Kitts a few years later, after which more than 150 years of periodic conflict resulted. The UK was finally recognized as the owner in 1787.

The two islands were settled and developed somewhat differently, despite their proximity to one another. St Kitts was made up of large land-holdings, founded on sugar cane cultivation. Today, sugar cane products, though of less importance than in the past, still account for more than 50 per cent of St Kitts' exports. The island's large farms also grow cotton, tobacco and coconuts for copra. Conversely, on Nevis, small plots are the rule, where high-quality cotton, fruits and vegetables are grown for local use, in addition to coconuts.

Besides tourism, which has become the nation's second most important industry next to agriculture, St Kitts has developed some light manufacturing, producing textiles, cigarettes and some electronic assembly.

MONTSERRAT

Montserrat, known as the Emerald Isle for both its Irish culture and its fertile, luxuriant appearance, lies just southeast of Nevis. A small volcanic island, only 18km (11 miles) long and 11km (7 miles) wide, it was at one time dominated by 914m-high (2999ft) Mount Chance; the peak is now merely a bump on the side of the huge Soufrière Hills volcano. At one time Montserrat had a population of 11,000 comprising mainly black slave descendants and a few expatriate British, Canadians and Americans, but the eruption of the volcano, which has occurred more or less continuously since 1995, has reduced the population by half. The southern portion of the island, including the capital Plymouth, was destroyed in 1997, after being evacuated. The once beautiful British dependent territory is now a study of man's struggle against the forces of nature. Its future remains uncertain.

atically up from the sea. The cloud-shrouded peaks are covered with grass-land and montane mist forests, below which is tropical rainforest. Mineral hot springs, especially around Nevis's chief town, Charlestown, have been a source of pleasure since colonial times, and the jungles harbour wild deer and Green Vervet Monkeys, brought by the French in the 1700s. Offshore, the clear waters are known for their wide variety of tropical fish and for unusually large stands of rare black coral. Scuba divers and

snorkellers consider the islands to be an exciting destination. Along the meandering coastlines are calm bays and silky sand beaches, and the islands' towns – the oldest British settlements in the Caribbean – have remarkable collections of lovely colonial buildings, unusual for their stone construction.

The islands, with their capital Basse-terre on St Kitts, gained independence in 1983. Having a mostly black population of 51,000 with all but 9000 of them on St Kitts, the islands' history followed a

Montserrat, once one of the Caribbean's most breathtaking islands, has lost large areas of its tropical vegetation to the eruption of the Soufrière Hills volcano.

With much of its economy destroyed together with its countryside, the residents are now reliant on the UK's financial support for survival.

Having a more unusual history than many of the Caribbean's islands, Montserrat, after being ignored by Columbus, became the region's only Irish Catholic colony when people sought to escape religious persecution by the Protestants in Europe. After the resident Caribs had been eradicated, African slaves were brought to the plantations in the 1630s. One hundred years later, Montserrat became one of the few English colonies to suffer a large-scale slave rebellion. When British troops quelled the insurrection, retribution was swift and complete: all the surviving rebels were executed. Today, they are regarded by locals as freedom fighters who gave their lives for the eventual emancipation of the slaves.

As in the other British Leeward colonies, the 17th and 18th centuries saw invasions from and continual strife with the French, which finally ended with the recognition of British sovereignty in 1783. However, the influence of France's occupations remain. Patois is one of the two languages spoken on the island, English being the other.

Prior to the volcanic disaster, Montserrat relied on tourism, which brought in nearly 30 per cent of the economy's revenues, some agriculture, and in the 1980s, on a growing offshore banking industry. Investigations by the British government resulted in many of the banks losing their licence for money-laundering and fraud. The entire industry was re-legislated as a result.

FRENCH WEST INDIES

The French colonies of the Caribbean, St Martin, St Barthélemy (or St Barts), Guadeloupe with its small, associated islands of La Désirade, Marie Galante,

and Ile des Saintes, and Martinique are among the loveliest isles in the Basin. All are located in the Lesser Antilles, on the border between the Atlantic Ocean and the Caribbean. St Martin and St Barts are the furthest north, in the Leewards chain; Guadeloupe is in the middle, at the beginning of the Windwards; and Martinique is the furthest south, in the mid-portion of the Windwards.

All of them green volcanic islands, they are blessed with coastlines that are indented with quiet bays and fringed by golden sands. The residents speak French or French patois, and their cultures reflect their French-influenced history, with cuisine, shopping and architecture clearly being European.

Historically, the islands all share a similar pattern. When Columbus came upon them in 1493 (the year he discovered much of the eastern Caribbean), he encountered fierce Carib Indians living there. Seeking to avoid the threat of violence, and deciding that the small islands were unlikely to have gold and silver, he passed them by, and they remained relatively undisturbed for the next 100 years. In the early 1600s, the French began settling them, island by island. The area soon became a battleground as struggles for dominance occurred with the English and the Dutch, and on several occasions, Spain. Ownership was traded back and forth for years.

As sugar cane and cacao plantations were developed, African slaves were imported in large numbers. When they were finally freed in 1848, thousands of indentured labourers were introduced to the islands from India to continue agricultural production.

By 1878, the various conflicts had been sorted out: the Caribs had been destroyed, the slaves were free people, and the islands had become colonies — departments of France, with residents having the rights of citizenship.

Today, there are two centres of government for the islands: Martinique is a department, as is Guadeloupe, which is also responsible for the administration

cent of its GNP derived from varied agriculture, but it has retained its remarkable natural beauty. Spectacular interior mountains, with Mount St Catherine reaching 840m (2756ft), are topped with thick rainforest.

Although Grenada is not a widely known destination, the main town of St George's, built around a prominence over a large bay, has a magnificent harbour view from virtually every spot in the town. The town's steep, hilly streets are crowded with 18th-century French colonial and English Georgian houses and buildings, painted in pastel shades.

The nearby Grand Etang National Park features a dramatic crater lake surrounded by rainforest, and hiking trails lead past tall *Ommier*, *Bois Canot* and *Blue Mahoe* trees draped with epiphytes and mosses. Higher up, a dimly lit mist forest flourishes beneath the clouds at the summit. Birds are plentiful, with many different hummingbirds, Chicken Hawks, and the rare Hook-billed Kite, found nowhere else in the world. As a final surprise, there is a troop of Mona Monkeys, who are now thriving in the mountains after having been introduced from Africa 300 years ago. Watersports enthusiasts enjoy windsurfing and parasailing, and divers can explore the huge Italian cruise ship *Bianca C*, which sank in 1961, besides the healthy coral reefs.

There is a unique aspect to Grenada's history: it is one of the few Caribbean islands to have experienced a modern military invasion. When the prime minister was murdered by Cuban-supported Communists after the 1983 elections, a joint Caribbean–US force occupied the island, jailed the perpetrators and expelled the communist foreign nationals. An interim government was established and subsequent elections were successful. Stability resulted and no further violence has arisen.

Besides agriculture, the growing economy has developed around fishing, manufactured food products (chocolate, sugar, rum, jams, coconut oil and lime juice) and tourism. With some 110,000 visitors and over 5400 yacht arrivals per year, the tourist industry is becoming increasingly important. The 98,000 residents, virtually all descendants of black and mulatto slaves, are steadily finding employment opportunities in tourism, as well as those in traditional agriculture.

BARBADOS

The independent nation of Barbados, the easternmost of the Caribbean islands, is actually situated in the Atlantic Ocean, just east of St Vincent. It is small, only 430km² (166 sq miles), formed of an undulating limestone plateau that rises up into low hills toward its northern end, with its highest point, Mount Hillaby, attaining a height of 340m (1116ft). Its capital, Bridgetown, is situated at the mouth of the Constitution River. Many of the historical buildings around its harbour have been restored, giving it a colonial character. Often referred to as 'Little England', Barbados retains the look and feel of England's 300-year uninterrupted rule. Because it is located 'upwind' of the rest of the Lesser Antilles chain, it was harder to reach than most of its neighbouring islands and therefore avoided the conflict and changing of hands over the years. After being discovered by the Portuguese in the 1500s and then settled by the English in 1627, the only other emigrants were African slaves and a Jewish colony from Pernambuco, which arrived in the mid-1600s.

The island, with its 259,000 residents (over 100,000 of whom live in Bridgetown), is the most densely populated in the Caribbean. The people are chiefly descendants of black slaves (80 per cent) with 4 per cent European and the balance mainly East Indian. Like most former British colonies, English is the official language, and Barbados has maintained a government that still recognizes the Queen, who is represented by her appointed governor general, as the chief of state. The governor general appoints the prime minister, who serves as the head of the local government. The legislative body is made up of a Senate that is set by the governor, and a House of Assembly elected by the populace.

Sinuous fire-eaters, backed by a calypso band, provide a favourite form of entertainment for tourists in Barbados, which lies east of the British Windwards.

The Barbados countryside looks much as it did throughout its colonial history. Virtually all of its rainforest was cleared long ago for the growing of sugar cane, which is still the predominant crop. Pretty homes and farms dot the landscape, surrounded by Poinciana, bougainvillea, hibiscus, and fruit trees. In recent years, more crop land has been devoted to growing vegetables and fruits for domestic consumption, but sugar cane cultivation still utilizes 60 per cent of the available land, and its products – sugar, molasses and rum – remain the major exports.

Commercial fishing is growing, for the waters around the island, at the confluence of the Caribbean and Atlantic, are prolific with both reef and oceanic species. A local dish made of Flying Fish is a speciality, while for export, crabs, lobsters and shellfish make up the majority. Recent discoveries of natural gas reserves promise to bring important revenues in the future, and a manufacturing sector has been established, producing electrical components, petroleum products and clothing.

Besides agriculture, tourism is the major industry. European and North American visitors enjoy the serenity of the green countryside and the long, golden beaches.

TRINIDAD AND TOBAGO

Often regarded as the most exotic islands of the Caribbean, Trinidad and Tobago lie just a few miles northeast of Venezuela. Once a part of the mainland during the ice age, the islands are home to the flora and fauna of both the Caribbean Basin and South America.

Nature still reigns supreme, with more than one-half of the land on both islands covered in primeval rain- and montane mist forest. Trinidad has unique wetland swamps, Caroni and Nariva, both acknowledged as national treasures. Visitors can cross vast water-filled plains – decorated with rushes, palms, Silk-

Paschimkaashi, a Hindu temple in Port of Spain, Trinidad. Hinduism arrived with the thousands of indentured Indian workers brought to the island in the 1800s.

cotton trees and giant lily pads – by kayak while marvelling at Howler Monkeys, Scarlet Ibis, parrots, and 400 other species of birds. In the rainforests of both islands, flowering trees are spectacular when in bloom: perfumed frangipani, the Pink and the Yellow Poui trees with their trumpet-shaped flowers, Pride of India, the beautiful Immortelle with its crimson blossoms, Jacarandas, Wild Poinsettias (the national flower of Trinidad and Tobago), and many others create a panorama of colours.

The two islands, after having become British colonies, joined together in 1889, then became an independent nation, the Republic of Trinidad and Tobago, in 1962. With a president chosen by the Electoral College from the Senate and House of Representatives, who serves as chief of state, and a prime minister (usually the head of the majority party) chosen by the president, the country is a parliamentary democracy. While the Senate is appointed by the president,

House of Representatives' members are chosen in free elections.

The island people are an exotic mix. Trinidad was discovered by Columbus on his third voyage in 1498, and settled first by the Spanish, then the French and British. Tobago was settled by the Dutch. African slaves were introduced to work the plantations, and when slavery ended, East Indians (from India) were brought to Trinidad in tens of thousands as indentured labourers. They eventually made up nearly one-half of the population. Of the present 1,130,000 people, most of them live in Trinidad. Trinidad's residents are 43 per cent black, 40 per cent East Indian, 14 per cent mulatto and 2 per cent Chinese, while Tobago's people are almost all black. As a result of this population difference, the lifestyles of the two islands are very different. Tobago is quiet, almost reclusive. It was, in fact, the model for Daniel Defoe's book, *Robinson Crusoe*. Conversely, Trinidad is a vibrant melting pot,

Folk dancing is popular in Tobago, and many hotels hold evening shows. The Tobago Folk Dancing Company, dedicated to the art, gives regular performances.

with Roman Catholic cathedrals next door to Hindu temples and Muslim mosques, while British, French and Spanish colonial buildings stand side by side along centuries-old streets. Muslims celebrate Eid ul Fitr in February/March and another festival during Muharran on the Islamic calendar (around July). In the autumn is the Hindu Festival of Lights, and biggest of all, is the *Carnaval de Mas* – 'Celebration of the Senses' – which has its roots in Catholicism. These pre-Lent festivities are usually held two days before Ash Wednesday. Trinidad's *Carnaval*, with its steel bands, costumed revellers and calypso, is believed to match Rio's world famous affair.

In Tobago, scuba diving has become a major activity, with pristine reefs that are highly regarded in the Caribbean. Hard and soft corals, crustaceans and shoals of bright fish occur in profusion.

The two islands, having more industry than most of their Caribbean neighbours – as a result of Trinidad's oil reserves –

carry out light manufacturing for export, and still produce cacao and coffee. Tourism is a growing resource; today, around 200,000 visitors each year are discovering for the first time the islands' exotic delights.

NETHERLANDS ANTILLES

Traditionally known as the Netherlands Antilles, these Caribbean colonies are now formally known as the Kingdom of the Netherlands. The group is comprised of Aruba, a self-governing island; the members of the Antillean Federation – Bonaire, Curaçao, Sint Maarten, Saba and Sint Eustatius; and the Netherlands. Aruba, Curaçao and Bonaire lie west-to-east, north of the Venezuelan coast, while Sint Maarten, Saba and Sint Eustatius lie north-to-south, in the Leeward Islands, between Anguilla and St Kitts.

Aruba, Bonaire and Curaçao, often called the ABC islands, are remnants of

the Venezuelan coastal cordillera (a series of parallel mountain ranges), and are flat and arid, with near-desert conditions. Cacti, thorn bushes, acacias and weirdly twisted *Divi-divi* trees are the main vegetation. Saba and Sint Eustatius, on the other hand, are green volcanic isles that rise up steeply from the sea. Sint Maarten is rather in-between, with rolling hills covered in low, drought-resistant shrubs and grasses.

Historically, the ABCs were discovered by the Spanish in 1499. Arawak Indians were settled there, although many of them were eventually shipped as slaves to plantations in the Dominican Republic. The Dutch arrived in the 1600s, and after some later conflicts with the British, eventually took full control of the islands during the 1700s and 1800s.

The northern group shared a similar history with the British Leewards in that they were discovered by Columbus (on his voyage in 1493), but they were settled and fought over by the English, Dutch and French. The indigenous Caribs were decimated, and the islands were eventually retained by the Dutch, when the Peace of Utrecht in 1713 ended the conflict between the Dutch and the English. Ultimately they split one island, with French St Martin on one half and Dutch Sint Maarten on the other.

The government today is the Dutch colonial model. The Queen of the Netherlands is the chief of state, and her appointed governor general represents her in the region. The local head of government is the prime minister, typically the leader of the majority party. The parliament, the *staten*, is elected by the populace. Aruba has its own prime minister and *staten*.

The other islands, through their membership in the Antillean Federation, are a federal parliamentary democracy whose seat of government is in Willemstad, Curaçao. Each island has its own Executive and Legislative Council, and the central *staten* is made up of elected representatives from each of the islands: 14 from Curaçao, three each from

This shuttered façade on Curaçao is a blend of Dutch and tropical architecture.

Bonaire and Sint Maarten, and one each from Saba and Sint Eustatius.

Efforts for the islands' complete independence were begun around 1954. Aruba was scheduled to become independent in 1996, but with the Netherlands in recent years reversing its support for this move, independence did not occur. Locally, moves have also been erratic; Curaçao was to have withdrawn from the Antillean Federation, but then voted to stay. Sint Maarten's vote to pull out was closer, with some 30 per cent of voters favouring separate status.

ARUBA

Aruba, the most western island, is only 193km² (75 sq miles) in size, and is located just west of Curaçao and north of Venezuela. It is flat, dry and hot, with only a few rolling hills, the highest point being a mere 188m (611ft). Because no plantations existed there, African slaves were not imported. As a result, the majority of its 68,000 people are mestizo – a mix of European and Caribbean

Indian. While Dutch is the official language, Papiamento (a mix of Dutch, Spanish, English, Portuguese and native Indian), is popularly spoken, along with Spanish and English.

Once the world's leading supplier of aloe products, Aruba's economy is now supported by oil refining and bunkering, though it is based chiefly on tourism: over 562,000 visitors arrive each year.

Tourists enjoy the mix of clear skies, hot sun and long, white-sand beaches. There are many luxury hotels, and divers and windsurfers are attracted in large numbers. The island's sand dunes, bird sanctuaries and wind-carved rock formations at places like Casibari provide unique sightseeing. Oranjestad, the capital, is a colonial delight with its pastel buildings and forts from the late 1700s.

CURAÇAO

Curaçao, just east of Aruba, is the largest of the Netherlands islands, being some 65km (40 miles) long and 11km (7miles) wide. It is relatively flat, with a

few low hills, and its coastline is indented with numerous deep bays. Like the other ABC islands, it is hot and arid, with desertlike vegetation, chiefly cacti and thorny shrubs. The buildings of its chief town, Willemstad, located on a large natural harbour along the south-western coastline, are a wonderful, tropical adaptation of 17th-century Dutch architecture in ice-cream hues.

Curaçao's mostly mestizo population of 170,000 is employed in oil refining – which accounts for nearly two-thirds of GNP – and tourism-related services. Some 220,000 arrivals, most of whom stay overnight, and 170,000 cruise ship passengers are generally from Holland (30 per cent), the USA and Venezuela (15 per cent each). Besides the upmarket hotels, casinos, deserted countryside, beaches and windsurfing, scuba diving is becoming one of the island's major drawcards. The waters are very clear, and steep walls are covered with corals and sponges. A collection of shipwrecks, the *Superior Producer* being a favourite, provide an eerie thrill.

BONAIRE

Bonaire lies east of Curaçao and is only slightly larger than Aruba, totalling 288km² (111 sq miles). Its 11,200 people live in small towns scattered around the dry, cactus-covered island. The main town of Kralendijk, with its sprinkling of Dutch colonial architecture, is home to only 1700 people. Because African slaves were introduced to Bonaire to labour in salt production – still an important export – the people today are generally of a European-Indian-African mix.

There are good hotels and several casinos to accommodate Bonaire's 67,000 annual visitors, but most come for the natural surroundings, on both land and sea. The north end of the island is occupied by the Washington–Slagbaai National Park, which provides refuge for over 190 species of birds, including over 15,000 Greater Flamingos, which are a breathtaking sight as they stand in vast, bright pink flocks, fields of colour

splashed across the sombre landscape. Nearly one-half of the island's visitors, however, are divers, and Bonaire is considered to be one of the Caribbean's favourite destinations. All the surrounding reefs are part of an island-wide marine park. Steep undersea cliffs, rich with sponges, corals and schools of fish, drop away just offshore. Under Kralendijk's main pier is a special dive: yellow sea horses, strange frogfish and friendly octopuses are all gathered in a small area. For snorkellers, the shallows around the tiny islet of Klein Bonaire – brilliant sands against transparent, turquoise water – are popular.

SINT MAARTEN

Sint Maarten, the northernmost of the Netherlands-owned islands, is in the midst of the British Leewards. The hilly island, which has lovely coves, harbours and beaches, is shared with the French colony of St Martin. The 32,000 residents of the Dutch side are descendants of European settlers and African slaves.

In the early 1990s, the local government was hit by a major scandal involving allegations of financial misdealings and the Netherlands increased its level of supervision as a result. This led to a strong separatist movement, but the efforts toward autonomy ultimately failed when the populace voted to retain the status quo.

The government was faced by an even more serious challenge in 1995 when the island was severely damaged by Hurricane Luis; hotels and the tourist infrastructure were destroyed, as were hundreds of yachts. Damages were ultimately placed at over a billion US dollars. Although most of the island's hotels missed the winter high season, repairs were undertaken in earnest, and rebuilding has been completed.

Because of too little rain, the islanders have historically been unable to do as well with agriculture as other Caribbean islands. What they have succeeded in is tourism. With over a million arrivals each year, Sint Maarten's half of the small

The Old Courthouse, dating back to 1793, in Philipsburg, Sint Maarten.

island is virtually lined with resorts and hotels. There are casinos and duty free stores, and watersport activities such as sailing, fishing and diving are popular. A well-known championship golf course is located at Mullet Bay. Cruise ships and yachts arrive at the capital of Philipsburg, located on a strip of land between Great Bay and Great Salt Pond.

SABA

Saba, just southwest of Sint Maarten, is one of the most unusual islands in the Caribbean. The entire land mass is an extinct volcano that rises straight up, on all sides, from the sea. The main town, The Bottom, sits inside the old crater, 800 stone steps up from the only harbour. The island's brightly painted homes, built amidst tropical greenery on the precipitous slopes, are picturesque. Rightly so, Saba has long been called 'Unspoiled Queen of the Caribbean'.

Hikers enjoy climbing to the top of Mount Scenery, whose highest point is 887m (2910ft). On the windward rising

slopes is deep rainforest with trees reaching heights of 9m (30ft), and palms and ferns growing thickly beneath them. Many birds, including the endemic Wood Hen, and land crabs and lizards can be seen. At the higher elevations of the island's interior, 4.5m (15ft) tree ferns become dominant and at the very top, mist forest contains stands of Mountain Mahogany. From the peak, the views are awesome, with green slopes falling steeply away to cobalt-blue ocean below.

Saba's clear, dramatic waters harbour steep undersea pinnacles which rise up from the depths and are enveloped in schools of swirling fish.

Although first discovered by Columbus in 1493, it was not settled for nearly 200 years, despite being a stopover for ships heading towards Puerto Rico. The fishing grounds on the Saba Banks and an abundance of fruit trees made the island popular for ships' crews living on sea rations. By the late 1600s, some 100 permanent settlers – half from

Holland, half from England — protected the island fiercely, and with the help of their slaves, prevented other settlers from coming ashore. The residents grew some sugar cane, coffee and cotton, and after 35 years of conflict, which took place during the late 1700s between the Dutch, English and French, Holland finally established clear ownership.

The local people today, one-half white, the other black, number only 1200. They continue with agriculture and fishing, and some local crafts — their fine, Spanish-derived embroidery, known as Saba lace, is famed in the region. Tourism, however, is becoming increasingly important, with 25,000 visitors coming to the small 13km² (5-sq-mile) island. They spend the majority of their time diving or hiking.

SINT EUSTATIUS

Sint Eustatius, more commonly known as Statia, is just south of Saba and 10km (6 miles) northwest of St Kitts. It is also small, at only 21km² (8 sq miles), and home to 2100 people. Its high point, at the island's southeast end, reaching a height of 601m (1972ft), is the peak of an extinct volcano called The Quill (after the Dutch word *kuil* for 'pit' or 'hole', likely referring to the crater itself). On the island's northeast end is the remnant of another volcano; the two are connected by a low-lying saddle of flat land.

Visitors are small in number but are drawn to this restful, somewhat dry island for its orchids, butterflies, and 50 different species of birds — which include the Bananaquit, Purple-throated Hummingbird, Slatey-tailed Trogon and Northern Jacana. Forest remains on only the most remote volcanic peaks. Offshore, diving is popular; many shipwrecks exist from the height of the island's maritime years. Most interesting, perhaps, is the town of Oranjestad itself, perched high on a crag overlooking the sea, its colonial buildings from the 1700s beautifully restored. Parts of the town look like historical relics plucked, intact, from the distant past.

Despite its small size, Statia has had an interesting history. Caught in the midst of the French, English and Dutch competition for colonies, it changed hands more than 20 times in the 150 years that followed Dutch settlement in 1636. The Dutch West Indies Company developed it into an agricultural and trading centre, which was so successful it became known as Golden Rock. In its heyday, the harbour of Oranjestad, the chief town, would usually be filled with hundreds of ships. Commerce involved the buying and selling of sugar cane, tobacco, rum and slaves.

During the American Revolution and the Civil War, the island became a staging point for blockade runners taking arms to the rebels of both wars. Lore has it that Fort Oranjestad's cannon salute to an arriving revolutionary war vessel was the first foreign acknowledgement of America's new-found freedom from the British.

Today, Statia is much quieter. The island does not compete well with others in the region for tourism, so the mainly black population depends on local agriculture and fishing, with few exports.

HONDURAS

Honduras, in Central America, lies between Guatemala and Nicaragua. Like Belize to the north, its history, especially in its eastern coastal region and offshore islands, is purely Caribbean. First discovered by Columbus in 1502, on his fourth voyage, and later visited by a series of Spanish explorers, including Hernán Cortés, Gil Gonzales Davila and Cristóbal de Olit, the area was difficult to tame, and it took many attempts to colonize the country. The thick, inaccessible jungle, the local Indian population, many of them descendants of the Mayan culture that had suddenly disappeared some 650 years before, and even competition and strife between the various Spanish factions all contributed to failed attempts to begin exploiting the area's extensive resources. The motivation was

strong, however: the forests were full of pine, oak and mahogany species. The fertile coastal plains could sustain virtually any crops, especially sugar cane, rice and tobacco. Offshore were large numbers of fish, lobster and shrimp. And, most importantly for the Spanish, rich deposits of minerals — gold, silver, tin, lead, zinc and coal — existed.

The Spanish immigrants enslaved the local Indians, who quickly died of disease and tough working conditions. It has been estimated that 90 per cent of the indigenous people perished within 20 years of Spain's arrival. In the recurring pattern of Caribbean history, slaves were imported from Africa to work the mines, plantations and timber operations. Once wealth began to be shipped out, new challenges arose. The Bay Islands, lying just 35km (21 miles) off the coast, became a hangout for English and Dutch pirates, who could easily raid Spanish galleons as they set out for Europe. At the same time, struggles began with the British, who occupied various portions of the country, including the Bay Islands, as late as 1852.

After 350 years of conflict, Honduras was granted independence from Spain in 1821. It established itself as a republic, and, although it is still one of the region's poorest countries, it has maintained a reasonable political stability, despite it being a refuge for Contra rebels during Nicaragua's internal strife in the 1980s. Today, it is governed by an elected president and National Assembly, with 18 provinces represented. Its capital is Tegucigalpa.

The 5.75 million people in Honduras are a manifestation of the country's history. Mainlanders are predominately Spanish-speaking mestizo (90 per cent), with 7 per cent still pure Indian. In certain places, there are Garífuna, who are black Carib descendants of the 5000 sent by the British from St Vincent to Roatán of the Bay Islands, off the Honduran coastline, after an uprising in 1797. The Islands, conversely, are populated by descendants of English pirates

and their black slaves, a few Lebanese, some Scotsmen who left the Caymans, and a small number of black Caribs.

The economy is largely agricultural, and is especially dependent on bananas, as well as coffee, citrus, pineapples and lumber. Revenues are also generated through the export of shrimp and lobster. Mining is important, and tourism, though not fully developed, is seen as a major opportunity for the future. The need for a broader economic base was underscored in the aftermath of Hurricane Mitch in 1998, which not only killed thousands of people, but also decimated the coastal banana crop, depriving the country of crucial revenues needed for redevelopment and repairs. This makes the ecotourists and divers, who frequent the Bay Islands of Roatán, Utila and Guanaja, even more important for the country's future.

On the mainland, the Caribbean coast is largely a long stretch of deserted golden sand. Just 40km (25 miles) inland, rainforest-covered mountains rise up, the highest reaching 2870m (9416ft). Within the forest are rivers for rafting, waterfalls, and ancient Mayan ruins (including Copán, the most ornately decorated of all the Mayan sites).

A remarkable collection of animal life also exists. There are jungle cats – Jaguars, Pumas, Ocelots, Jaguarundi and Margays – and some 700 species of brilliantly plumaged birds. Besides the toucans, macaws and parrots, are other exotic birds such as the Guatemalan Ivorybill, Rufous-tail Jacamar, Jabiru Stork, Great Curassow and Black-collared Hawk. Reptiles include boas and the deadly *Fer-de-lance*.

BAY ISLANDS

The Bay Islands are a joy, a step back to gentler times. Beaches are unspoiled, hills are covered with forests of wild fruit trees, oaks, pines and bamboo, and offshore, remarkable reefs and drop-offs feature coral, sponges and fish. Roatán offers a unique opportunity to dive with dolphins, and Utila is one of the only places in the Caribbean where the largest fish in the sea, Whale Sharks – attaining 10.5m (35ft) in length – can be seen on a regular basis.

All in all, Honduras together with the Islands is an ecotourist treasure not fully discovered. In the meantime, current visitors largely have this country to themselves, and experiences offered genuinely tread the narrow bridge between tourism and real-life adventure.

An enchanting waterfall cascades from a cliff on Guanaja, one of the Bay Islands which lie north, off the Honduran coast. Called the Isle of Pines by intrepid seafarer Christopher Columbus, Guanaja is popular among hikers and divers.

Waterfront buildings in the Belizean capital of Belize City. Offshore is one of the world's longest barrier reefs and the Caribbean Basin's only true coral atolls.

BELIZE

Belize, just north of Honduras and Guatemala on the Central American coastline, is bordered by the Caribbean Sea to the east, and has a high spine of mountains rising to 1160m (3806ft) in its interior. It is the type of place for which the term ecotourism was invented. It retains 80 per cent of its original forest, and its barrier reef is the second longest in the western hemisphere, having some 295km (180 miles) of reefs, cays and the only true coral atolls in the Caribbean. Places like Ambergris Cay, Glover's Reef, Lighthouse Reef and the Turneffe Islands are known worldwide for their palm-fringed sandy isles, majestic coral structures and undersea walls, and their rich variety of marine life.

In San Ignacio, Chiquibul and many other areas around the countryside, there are fabulous cavern systems, most of them containing artefacts from the ancient Mayan civilization. The Maya Mountains rise steeply above the lowland coastal plains, covered by virgin rainforest of White Mahogany, Banak, Caribbean Pine, Sapodilla, Colume Palms, oaks, and many other varieties of tropical vegetation. With 30 per cent of

the country's land set aside as preserves, Belize is determined to protect the 250 species of orchid, 500 bird species, and countless mammals, reptiles, amphibians, and insects that thrive in the jungles, marshes and rivers. A nature hike may reveal Howler Monkeys, anteaters, toucans, boa constrictors, gaudy Leaf Frogs and iridescent Blue Morpho Butterflies (one of 700 butterfly species to be found there). Less likely to be seen, but common, are Jaguars, Ocelots, Tapirs, and Spider Monkeys.

Given its colonial history, Belize is fortunate to have its natural environment so well-preserved, for while it was not cleared for extensive plantations, it was intended for lumbering. No real impact was made, perhaps because the area was so rugged, and relatively little of the original forest was destroyed. Belize was discovered by Columbus on his fourth voyage, in 1502. He found the remnants of the Mayan culture, which had mysteriously declined after having reached its peak in 300AD. The huge temple ruins in places like Altún Há and Nomul were undoubtedly as impressive to the early explorers as they are to visitors today.

When the English settled the area and began logging in 1631, using African

slave labour to toil in the dense forests, a conflict with the Spanish began that would continue on and off for nearly 200 years. Spain was finally forced out of the area in the 1820s. After several uprisings in the years that followed, the slaves – more than 75 per cent of the population – were emancipated in 1838. In 1862 Belize, then called British Honduras, became a British colony.

The government, after independence in 1981, became a parliamentary democracy like most of the former British colonies. The Queen is the titular chief of state, and represented by a governor general who appoints the prime minister and the Senate. The National Assembly is elected by popular vote.

The people of Belize today show the mark of history in their racial mix: 44 per cent are mestizo, 30 per cent mulatto, 11 per cent pure Maya and 7 per cent are Garífuna (black Caribs deported from St Vincent by the British).

The country's immense ecological resources have made tourism the second largest industry, behind agriculture, which focuses on sugar cane, citrus and bananas. Seafood exportation, especially shrimp and Spiny Lobster, is also important, with the mining of dolomite a growing revenue producer.

YUCATAN PENINSULA

Just north of Belize, the Yucatán peninsula juts out into the Caribbean Sea, coming to within 229km (142 miles) of the western tip of Cuba.

While most of Mexico would not be considered to fall under 'the Caribbean', the coastline encompassed in the state of Quintana Roo, extending from the Belize border to the Yucatán's northern tip, generally is. It shares similarities with much of the rest of the Basin, especially in terms of history, interaction with the European colonial powers and the influences of the Caribbean Sea itself.

The Yucatán does have some distinct differences in that the majority of the people living there are not descended

from slaves and colonial immigrants but from the indigenous Indian race. Culturally, the area was the birthplace of the Olmecs as far back as 1000BC, followed by the Maya in 300AD and the Toltecs 600 years later. Advanced civilizations, they developed mathematics, accurate calendars, and a written language. Their temples and fortifications still stand, scattered in jungles and perched on seaside cliffs. Ruins, like those at Tulūm, near the small town of Akumal, are impressive – and quite dramatic.

Offshore, reefs and undersea walls run continuously for over 280km (174 miles). The small island of Cozumel, one of the Yucatán's most visited destinations, is among the favoured Caribbean dive sites. The famed Palancar Reef is a marvellous collection of coral mounds, canyons and sheer walls, home to an astounding collection of fish, such as groupers, jacks, tuna and snappers.

For serious adventurers, the jungled countryside is also the location of one of the world's most complex systems of underwater caves. Divers swim thousands of feet into these dark passageways, which were formed by rainwater dissolving the soft limestone substrate over the eons. To add to the fascination, the cenotes – surface openings to the cave systems – were often the sites of Mayan habitation, because they were constant sources of fresh water. Through the centuries, a great number of artefacts were thrown into the deep pools (it is believed that these were offerings to appease the gods), and they are frequently found, fully preserved.

The peninsula supports an impressive collection of wildlife, particularly birds. Throughout the region are flocks of Wild Canaries, Blue Warblers, parrots, and macaws. In the thick mainland forests are Agouti, anteaters, Peccaries, and jungle cats, such as Jaguars and Ocelots. Along the coastlines, turtles, flamingos and, rarely, Manatees can be spotted.

When the Spanish explorer Hernán Cortés found the area in 1519, he began swiftly to obliterate the culture he had

A view from San Miguel, the main town of Cozumel, off the Yucatán peninsula.

discovered. He was soon followed by zealot Franciscan friars who set out to eliminate any trace of the Mayan past, which they considered to be the work of the devil. They systematically destroyed temples, altars and most of the codices that recorded the intricacies of Mayan language and science.

Pirates also frequented the coast, building hideouts on small islands like Cozumel and Isla Mujeres, and periodically looting local settlements.

In the 1840s, when the peaceful Mayan descendants finally rebelled, a Spanish army was brought in which either killed them or shipped them – some 200,000 – into slavery. For a hundred years after, Mayan guerrillas waged war in the jungles.

The Quintana Roo region finally found peace and became a Territory of Mexico in 1934, and with the city of Mérida its capital, it was admitted as a state of the Republic of Mexico in 1974.

Today, the people are predominantly mestizo or pure Maya. In all of Mexico, pure Indians still make up 15 per cent of the population. It is estimated that one-half of the pure-bloods live in the Yucatán. Many make their living out of simple farming and fishing, but tourism has become the sustaining industry for most of the area.

One of the more interesting attractions in the Yucatán is the tourist city of Cancún. As part of a plan by the Mexican government to develop tourism, a small sandbar along a deserted stretch of coast was selected and in only four years a city – designed purely to provide pleasure for vacationers – was built.

Surrounded by sparkling beaches and an aquamarine ocean, the collection of luxury hotels, restaurants, bars, and entertainment centres has become one of the Caribbean's most successful resort areas, receiving millions of visitors annually, particularly from the USA.

THE BAHAMAS & TURKS AND CAICOS

The islands of the Bahamas and the Turks and Caicos, the northernmost of the Caribbean region, are actually not in the Caribbean Sea at all but lie in the tropical Atlantic Ocean. The two island nations, geographically appearing as one continuous chain, were formed by coral growth along the North American continental shelf. Washed by the nutrient-rich flow of the Gulf Stream, the waters around the islands are alive with fish, lobster and conch. The popularity of the scuba diving, game fishing and glorious white sand beaches among visitors has made tourism the most important economic factor for both islands.

The Bahamas, site of Columbus's first landing in the New World, are made up of nearly 700 islands and 2000 small cays, scattered across huge shallow banks that glow turquoise under the tropical sun. Once a British colony, the now independent people of the archipelago lead a comfortable lifestyle and have a high standard of living. They live in a few rather metropolitan cities like Nassau and Freeport, and scores of tiny villages on many of the small islands.

Upscale Nassau and Freeport vibrate with energy. Cruise ships and luxury yachts fill the harbours, and sumptuous resorts and casinos cater to travellers from around the world. Discos blare soba and reggae music, and fine restaurants serve cuisine of every description. Out on the 'Family Islands', as the

smaller islands are often called, life has a much different style and tempo. Small resorts provide the tranquillity of sand, sea and sun, away from the hustle of modern civilization. Local seafoods, caught fresh from nearby waters, are the cuisine of choice, while the warmth of the local people is irrepressible.

At the southern extent of the Bahamas, the Turks and Caicos Islands, 40 in all and only eight of which are inhabited, are remote and quiet, and appear scarcely touched by modern times. The dry islands, covered with wild scrub, sit low on the blue Atlantic Ocean, fringed by brilliant white sand. Formed around a huge lagoon, the islands are a refuge for bird life that thrives on protected, unmolested small islands and cays.

Historically a centre for salt production, the small independent nation now benefits chiefly from its rich waters. The Turks Island Passage, which allows flow between the Atlantic and the Caribbean Sea, creates an amazingly healthy marine ecosystem that supports majestic coral reefs and prolific fish life. One of the only whale calving grounds in North American waters, the Silver Banks, lies just to the southeast. Scuba divers and fishermen hold the islands among their favourite off-the-beaten-track destinations. But remote does not mean uncivilized in the case of the Turks and Caicos, and its resorts and hotels are exclusive and upmarket.

A simple cross (above left) *commemorates Christopher Columbus's first landing in the New World, at San Salvador in the southern Bahamas, and a statue of the intrepid seafarer* (left) *stands in front of Government House in the capital, Nassau, on New Providence Island. The modern Supreme Court building* (above) *retains the islands' traditional colonial style.*

Government House (opposite top), *built in 1801, commands a view of Nassau from the top of Mount Fitzwilliam Hill. The neoclassical mansion is the residence of the Queen of England's representative, the governor general. From Government House's broad steps* (opposite bottom), *visitors watch the changing of the guard, a ceremony from British colonial times. Having gained independence on 10 July 1973, the Bahamas are an independent member of the Commonwealth and utilize a government and school system based upon the British model.*

PREVIOUS PAGES
PAGE 60: *Elaborate celebration mask displayed in the Junkanoo Museum at the Prince George Wharf in Nassau harbour.*
PAGE 61: *The outer islands of the Bahamas have some of the world's most pristine beaches, quiet and untouched.*

Elaborately columned hotel grounds (left) *in Nassau, New Providence. Once a refuge for Caribbean pirates, Nassau's harbour* (right) *is now a popular port for cruise ships. Under the bridge connecting Nassau with Paradise Island, Potter's Cay's stalls sell fresh seafood, woven straw items and luscious fruits such as these papayas, mangoes, pineapples, and coconuts* (below). *For sunworshippers, there are beach umbrellas* (below centre) *at the water's edge on Paradise Island and Hobie Cat sailing* (below right), *on nearby Cable Beach. For ultimate solitude, long deserted beaches like those on Cat Island* (bottom) *are unmatched.*

Transparent waters off San Salvador (top) are a snorkeller's delight, and scuba divers (left) explore Atlantis Road – the remains of the lost continent of Atlantis, according to legend – off Bimini. A Slipper Lobster (above).

On their way to Easter services, Bahamian children (opposite top) grow up in a society that places a great deal of importance on religion. Churches of a number of denominations, many dating from the early 1800s, exist throughout the islands, and include Presbyterian, Roman Catholic, Anglican and Greek Orthodox.

Church services are celebrated with a joy and vigour characteristic of the Bahamian culture. Ladies attending services (opposite bottom) prepare to spend the morning in song and prayer. The chants and choral singing of many faiths take on special life in a society so infused with African musical traditions.

On remote Cat Island, named after pirate Arthur Catt, the Hermitage (above) is a miniature replica of an Italian monastery. Built atop Mount Alvernia, the highest point in the Bahamas (64m; 210 ft), the proportions of the Hermitage are perfect for children.

The small church on Walker's Cay (right) is used by visitors and locals alike. The tiny cay, the northernmost point of the Bahamas, is occupied by a resort, long considered one of the world's top big-game fishing locations. Locals commute to work – and to services – on small boats.

Cuba

Cuba, the Caribbean's largest island – covering 114,524km² (44,218 sq miles) – is also one of its most intriguing. No other island in the Basin has the diversity of geography, climate, flora and fauna that Cuba has with its mountains, plains and endless stretches of remote coastline.

Its political history, however, is what most sets it apart from the other islands in the region. Like its eastern neighbours, Hispaniola and Puerto Rico, Cuba was discovered by Columbus and developed by Spain. Not only was it used for sugar plantations, as with the other islands in the Basin, it also had considerable mineral and forestry resources. Spain carefully protected the island and maintained ownership until 1898, when it was granted to the USA as a result of the Spanish American War.

In the early 20th century, Cuba's capital Havana developed into one of the world's most exciting cities. With its music, dance, casinos and sumptuous hotels, the city became synonymous with the pursuit of pleasure. When the Castro-led communist revolution took place in 1959, however, Havana – and the country as a whole – abruptly changed. With one of the world's most strict communist regimes in power, the trappings of luxury and free-wheeling capitalism quickly disappeared. For the next 35 years, the country, with considerable economic support from the USSR, maintained a stable, well-educated society.

With the political and economic changes that have occurred in the USSR, and the subsequent loss of financial support for Cuba, the island and its people are now facing a challenging future.

Cuba is, in many ways, an enigma. Opening its doors to tourism for the first time in many years, the island has incredible natural beauty and its architecture, music and dance reflect its colonial past. However, it has a crumbled infrastructure, its transportation system is poor and its hotels have long since lost their glitter of the 1950s. The decadent, bourgeois values so spurned by the revolution were, in fact, the very structures upon which the country's immensely lucrative tourism had been built. Today, as Cuba struggles to rebuild its tourist appeal, it is ironic that many of those same institutions are re-emerging and creating new difficulties: present-day Cuban society is one in which waiters and prostitutes, the recipients of visitors' cash, earn more than doctors and other highly educated professionals.

As the world discovers the island nation's true innate appeal, however, it seems likely that its fortunes will rise. Visitors are discovering scuba diving and marvellous sightseeing opportunities, low prices and a warm welcome from people in dire need of the monetary worth the visitors bring. However, the ultimate direction the country's current half-capitalist, half-socialist culture will take remains to be seen.

ESCOGER EL CAMINO
DE LA RESISTENCIA SIGNIFICA
QUE NO SOLO SEREMOS CAPACES
DE RESISTIR, SINO TAMBIEN DE VENCER

George Town (above) *is the capital of the Cayman Islands. The historic town has maintained its traditional charm, while managing to entertain hundreds of thousands of tourists each year. Behind its quiet exterior, George Town is one of the most active financial centres in the world, with over 600 banks in residence. Grand Cayman's Seven Mile Beach* (left) *is one of the most favoured throughout the Caribbean.*

PREVIOUS PAGES
PAGE 92: *The Dunn's River Falls in the town of Ocho Rios, Jamaica.*
PAGE 93: *Flamingo Tongue Shells, Cayman Brac.*

THE CAYMAN ISLANDS & JAMAICA

The Cayman Islands and Jamaica, lying near each other just south of Cuba, are among the Caribbean's most well visited tourist areas. Connected politically at various times in their past under British rule, the Cayman Islands were originally settled by British colonists from Jamaica. Today, however, geographically and socially their dissimilarities are far more profound.

The Cayman Islands, which have remained a British colony, are three flat coral isles – Grand Cayman, Cayman Brac and Little Cayman – which have formed on an undersea ridge along the edge of the precipitous Cayman Trench. The gentle climate and moderate rainfall keep the islands green, with day after day of tropical sunshine. The resorts appeal to an upscale market, especially divers, who regard the islands' crystal-clear waters as the best the Caribbean has to offer.

A well-heeled region, the Cayman Islands enjoy the Caribbean's highest standard of living and a cosmopolitan culture that retains much of British style and tradition. In a clean and modern environment, fine restaurants and shopping centres carry goods from around the globe. Despite the success of the islands' tourism, their status as the fifth largest financial centre in the world is the economy's most significant factor – tax-free living is a reality for resi-

dents and visitors alike, while assets have attained almost US$6 billion.

The independent nation of Jamaica is a large, mountainous island formed by volcanic action, covered with tangled forests and crisscrossed by rivers. The Blue Mountains and central highlands are where much of the country's natural rainforest still thrives, while the Dunn's River Falls in Ocho Rios – one of Jamaica's three major tourist towns, along the north coast – is a famous local attraction. Beyond the island's agricultural exports, tourism is its most important industry, with cruise ships and resorts bringing over a million visitors each year. These visitors enjoy the beaches, beautiful countryside, mountains and waterfalls – as well as the riotous, party atmosphere that attracts young people from around the world.

Jamaica's large resident population – over 2.5 million people – is either crowded into the sprawling city of Kingston or lives in small agricultural and coastal areas around the country.

Perhaps best known for its music, the island is the home of reggae, brought into world focus during the 1970s by Jamaican musicians Bob Marley and, later, Peter Tosh. At the roots, reggae is the political expression of its Rastafarian faith, reflecting the needs of its people for increased opportunity and an improved economic situation.

Guantánamo, the province on Cuba's extreme eastern tip, is remote and scarcely populated, with a scattering of small villages (left). The area's major settlement, Baracoa, is an ancient town in the shadow of El Yunque, 'the anvil', a huge, flat-topped mesa that was first seen from offshore by Columbus in 1492.

Stately Royal Palms outside Baracoa (below) have numerous uses: the fronds make excellent thatch, the green portion of the trunk is used in the making of waterproof roofing material, the trunk itself is high quality timber, and the seeds are used to feed pigs.

Trinidad's Old Town has a marvellous collection of colonial styles. There are relatively few vehicles in an area that lends itself chiefly to walking. The buildings along this quiet street (opposite top) *feature* rejas, *wooden window screens made of lathe-turned rods.*

The Spanish tiles and intricate window and door coverings are common elements in the island's traditional architecture, manifested in this Trinidad residence with its classic Cuban-colonial ambience (opposite bottom).

With a population of only 38,000, Trinidad (above) remains one of Cuba's most comfortable cities. A free port in the late 1700s, it accumulated great wealth, and became known for its beautiful homes as well as its talented artisans, who worked with intricate lace, ceramics, silver, and gold.

Plaza Mayor (right), *the heart of the original settlement, has a beautiful park and is surrounded by a cathedral and several museums; the buildings were once the ornate homes of wealthy citizens.*

The waters around the Cayman Islands are noted for their warm temperature, astounding clarity and calmness (right), *and for their vibrant coral reefs teeming with life – factors that have helped the islands develop a reputation for being one of the most popular diving and snorkelling destinations in the world. The mood is idyllic on Cayman Brac* (below), *which is frequented by divers and bird-watchers. Its inland Salt Water Pond is a refuge for wading birds and its reefs, which begin in shallow water just offshore, have large schools of snappers and other fish.*

Due to the success of the Cayman Turtle Farm's hatch and release pro-gramme, local reefs again have a large population of turtles. The islands' turtles had been almost eradicated by hunting during colonial times. A scuba diver encounters a Hawksbill Turtle (left) near Cayman Brac.

Divers play with a school of Southern Stingrays (below) at Grand Cayman's most unique dive site, Stingray City, where feeding creates a fascinating and most exhilarating encounter.

A Rough File Clam (below), although it usu-ally remains hidden in crevices on the Little Cayman reefs, can swim surprisingly well when attempting to escape from a predator. In shallow sandy areas, colonies of Yellow-head Jawfish (bottom) live in burrows on the sea floor. Males carry the fertilized eggs in their mouths, carefully incubating them until they hatch.

A Jamaican banana plantation worker (left) balances a large stem of bananas on her head. The island, once the world's largest producer of the fruit, exports over 240,000 tons each year. The Great River (above) flows through wilderness lands and empties into the sea at beautiful Montego Bay which, besides Ocho Rios and Negril, is one of Jamaica's three main tourist centres.

Named for an Arawak priestess, the Martha Rae River emerges at Windsor Caves and flows to Oyster Bay. Its 90-minute raft trip (left) is one of Jamaica's most interesting river runs.

Away from the busy cities and tourist areas, Jamaica's interior is quiet and bucolic, with farming the main activity (right).

*Hand-woven berets in the traditional Rastafarian colours (above) are
displayed for sale in Montego Bay. The Rastafarian faith is founded on
the premise that Africans were one of the chosen people of God – one
of the twelve tribes of Israel. Adherents of the religion believe that
Jamaica, where they are now exiled, is Babylon.*

A local Rastafarian (right top) *wears his hair in traditional dreadlocks style, one expression of the religion's belief in living naturally. Other aspects of the Rastafarian lifestyle involve the smoking of ganja, or marijuana, and the playing of reggae – the lyrics express their political views, in songs about poverty and oppression.*

On popular Montego Bay, paddle-skis for hire (above) *line the beach, awaiting the tourists' arrival. With over a million visitors each year, Jamaica ranks third in the Caribbean, and the over US$965 million in revenues produced annually makes tourism the island's most important industry. Its all-inclusive luxury resorts specialize in upper income groups, including singles, honeymooners and families.*

HAITI, DOMINICAN REPUBLIC & PUERTO RICO

Located in the Greater Antilles, Haiti and the Dominican Republic, which share the large island of Hispaniola, and Puerto Rico, lying just to the east, have a similar geological and historical past. These high mountainous isles, formed by volcanic activity, also feature large karst areas, where ancient, coral-line limestone substrate has been weathered by percolating rainwater, creating hills, depressions and cavern systems. Haiti is the most mountainous of the three, although the highest peak, Pico Duarte, is in the Dominican Republic.

The size of the islands led the Spanish, whose main interest was gold, silver and other metals, to colonize them, after ignoring many smaller islands less likely to have such natural resources. The indigenous Arawak Indians, forced into slave labour, were fast eradicated, to be replaced by African slaves. With Santo Domingo in the Dominican Republic the New World's original permanent city, and Haiti and Puerto Rico settled soon after, colonial history infuses these islands and is reflected in their cultures today.

After Spanish colonization, the Dominican Republic suffered incursions by the French, English and Haitians, and fell into more than 300 years of invasion and revolt; it did not reach social stability until the latter part of the 20th century. Today, the country is earning a place as a tourist favourite. Its coastline is dotted with small towns whose plazas contain buildings from the 1500s, their stone and masonry maintained to look much as it did when Spanish explorers sailed the waters. The country's natural beauty is breathtaking too, with rainforest in the highlands and a bountiful ocean enjoyed by divers, snorkellers and fishermen.

Haiti was soon taken from the Spanish by France and developed into a plantation colony. It, too, suffered its own series of slave revolts and rebellions, which culminated in dictatorial governments that persisted until modern times. It is now a populous country, struggling for economic stability on lands largely stripped of forest and depleted of nutrients. The numerous small farms and garden plots of this poor agricultural society cultivate crops chiefly for local consumption. An exotic culture has nonetheless produced art treasures and the mysticism of voodoo.

Puerto Rico, which remained relatively stable under Spanish rule until it was ceded to the USA in 1898, today is a marvellous mix of natural splendours, its colonial heritage, and modern metropolitan living. One of the Caribbean's leading tourist destinations, its status as a US territory has ensured economic opportunities beyond those of most neighbouring islands. Modern hotels and resorts co-exist with houses built in colonial times, while mountain rainforest and golden beaches remain unspoiled, despite the growth of population and industry.

A Haitian basket seller (left) *on the way to the capital city, Port au Prince, where locally produced goods are sold along the roadside. In Haiti's mountain areas* (right), *farmers work the land by hand, and a shelter* (above) *provides some shade for the field workers. Poor soil and a lack of modern farming techniques exacerbate Haiti's problems of feeding and providing employment for its large population. Even irrigation must often be attempted without access to the most basic machinery* (below).

PREVIOUS PAGES
PAGE 102: *A picturesque street in Old San Juan, Puerto Rico.*
PAGE 103: *Expressive local art on a bus in Haiti.*

Voodoo priests take part in a ritual parade (above). *Voodoo, based on an ancient West African religion, remains a powerful force in everyday Haitian life. Harmony must be maintained with nature, the dead, and powerful spirits called* loas, *through offerings and animal sacrifice. Any attempt to use the magic of the* loas *for evil or personal gain is considered malevolent, and those who carry out the practice are called* bokors, *or sorcerers.*

To commune with the loas, *they need to be induced to take control of people's bodies. Using drumming, feverish dancing and singing, a woman goes into the trance necessary for this possession* (right).

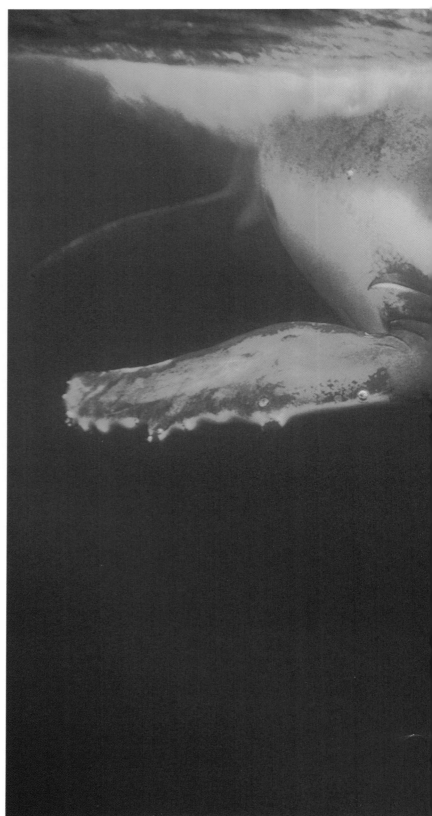

Off the Dominican Republic's northeast coast, the Silver Banks area is a calving ground for majestic Humpback Whales. The huge marine mammals, reaching 18m (59ft) in length and weighing as much as 30 tons, feed in the cold waters of the Arctic during most of the year, but come to the Banks from January through March to both mate and give birth. Calves are about 4.3m (14ft) long when born, and suckle for up to 10 months.

The reduction in whaling around the world has resulted in a resurgence of this beautiful species, which was at one time well on its way to extinction. It is estimated that some 5000 to 6000 Humpbacks are found in the northern Atlantic. The whales are relatively accepting of humans, and allow snorkellers to approach them closely. A number of boats make regular snorkelling trips to the Silver Banks area.

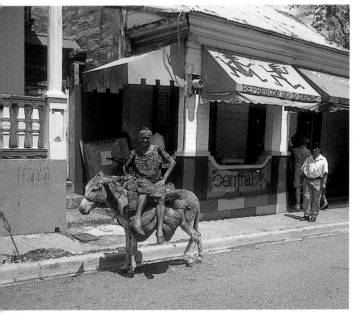

Merengue, *the traditional musical style of the Dominican Republic, is played by a three-piece group* (opposite top) *termed* perico ripiao. *The musicians' instruments are an accordion, drum and a* guira *scraped by a metal rod.*

Using a donkey as a means of transport, a local woman ambles down a village street (opposite bottom left). *On a nearby beach, local art is displayed for sale* (opposite bottom right).

A country stall (above) *in the Dominican Republic's mountain region sells a variety of local fruits. Hardwoods from these highland forests are used by artisans to produce fine carvings* (right) *for sale to tourists.*

111

The fortress of San Felipe (left), *in Puerto Plata, was the first one to be built in the Caribbean. Made of heavy stone blocks, it guarded the city throughout years of invasion by the English, French, pirates, and Haitians. In the mountains outside the city, the world's largest deposits of amber – fossilized tree resin – were discovered; today, Puerto Plata is known for its exquisite amber jewellery trade.*

A fisherman mends fish traps (below) *at the Scott's Head fishing village. Several such villages, among them Palmar de Ocoa and Bayahibe, continue to practise traditional fishing techniques, but have begun to accommodate tourists as well, who enjoy the rustic atmosphere.*

Although two-thirds of the Dominican Republic's virgin rainforest was eradicated after the arrival of Columbus, the government has now protected 67 different areas, preserving the remaining natural resources for the future. Highland rainforest around the mountain, Pico Duarte (above), contains mahogany trees, ferns and over 100 species of orchid.

The forests and beaches of the Dominican Republic are home to many of the New World's 857 species of palm, including these Coconut Palms (right).

Guarding the entrance to San Juan, which has served as Puerto Rico's harbour since it was built in 1591, the fortress of San Felipe del Morro (above) *is the city's most famous landmark. Its strategic position helped defend Spain's Caribbean holdings against the English, French and Dutch for hundreds of years.*

The El Morro lighthouse (left) *still guides ships into San Juan's harbour. Representative of the true essence of San Juan, it is a marriage of old and new, colonial and modern.*

Constructed in 1772 to protect San Juan's landward side, Fort San Cristóbal *(right)* is a large structure made up of five independent units that are connected by dry moats and a system of underground tunnels. In the fort's courtyard, visitors enjoy reenactments of Spanish military ceremonial traditions *(below)*. The presence of San Juan's forts spared the city the frequent sacking and capture that plagued most of the Caribbean settlements.

VIRGINS, BRITISH LEEWARDS & FRENCH WEST INDIES

The island groups normally included in the Lesser Antilles are the Virgin Islands (US and British); the British Leewards, which include Anguilla, Barbuda, Antigua, St Kitts and Nevis, and Montserrat; and the French West Indies, made up of St Martin, St Barthélemy, Guadeloupe and Martinique. As a whole, they are small, lovely islands, the favourite haunts of yachtsmen and sun-worshippers. Historically, they are similar in that they were discovered by Columbus but were not considered particularly important to the Spanish. However, the English, French and Dutch colonized them and fought over them for centuries.

Strategically, they form the division between the Caribbean Sea and the Atlantic Ocean, in the area where ships entered the Caribbean on the main routes from Europe. This made the islands prime hunting grounds for pirates – and therefore subject to the building of military fortresses. Perhaps their most important use, however, was for the growing of sugar cane. With most of the islands having been created from volcanic forces, they tend to have extremely rich soils. With a few exceptions, they are also generally located in a zone of ample rainfall, in the immediate path of the hurricane belt. They were therefore perfect for development into agricultural economies. For many of the islands, agriculture remains a chief financial mainstay, with bananas having replaced sugar cane as the major crop. Tourism has become the other economic driver, and islands like St Martin and Martinique, in the French West Indies, are among the Caribbean's most successful holiday destinations, while the US and British Virgin Islands are among the most sought-after yachting venues in the world.

Several of these island groups have not rallied in the drive for independence, as has occurred in much of the rest of the Basin. The US Virgin Islands remain a territory of the USA; the British Virgin Islands, Anguilla and Montserrat remain British dependencies; and the French West Indies remain overseas departments of France. This has kept much of the area's colonial nature intact – in fact, Martinique could be a slice of Paris transposed in the tropics.

Some of the islands have immense natural beauty. Nevis, Guadeloupe and Martinique, especially, retain much natural vegetation, with rainforest and long, deserted shorelines. The region's volcanic history – as well as today's active volcanism – are still much in evidence. Montserrat has experienced eruptions since 1995, with much of the island now uninhabitable. On Martinique, one of the island's most intriguing tourist attractions is the ruined city of Saint Pierre, which was completely destroyed by a massive eruption in 1902. Of the 30,000 people who were killed, one survivor was left in the entire city.

PREVIOUS PAGES
PAGE 118: *Fishing boats in Dieppe Bay, St Kitts, part of the British Leeward Islands.*
PAGE 119: *Brightly painted building in Antigua, British Leeward Islands.*

Translucent seas in the British Virgin Islands: snorkellers take advantage of the crystal waters around Cooper Island (top left); *gigantic granite rocks at The Baths, Virgin Gorda* (top right); *and sailboats – their spinnakers catching the wind – take part in a regatta* (above).

The quiet beach at Cane Garden Bay (top) is often considered to be one of the most lovely on Tortola, in the British Virgin Islands; the Callwood Rum Distillery nearby still makes rum using methods dating back to the 18th century. A view across to the small island, Guana (above), which lies to the north of Tortola. Privately owned, its small resort offers the ultimate in exclusive vacationing. Also a wildlife sanctuary, it has a resident flock of Greater Flamingos. The harbourside at Frenchman's Cay (above); this small island situated opposite the ferry docks at West End, Tortola, has an upscale resort, a marina and shops, as well as a number of good beaches.

Beautiful Trunk Bay (above), at St John in the US Virgin Islands, is St John's favourite beach. Here, the National Parks Service maintains a snorkelling trail, which, for those who are experiencing the thrills of the underwater world for the first time, proves to be a wonderful place to start. On

St Croix, south of St John, a building in Christiansted (below left) reflects the elegant style of the island's Dutch heritage. A catamaran beaches at Buck Island, St Croix (below); the waters here form an underwater national park, with an abundance of bright fish and corals.

A street scene on the US Virgin island of St Thomas (below). The island not only has beautiful waters and beaches, but also some of the Caribbean's best duty-free shopping. A smiling resident of St Thomas (above); most are English-speaking US citizens, although many also speak a West Indian dialect influenced by English, Danish, Dutch, French, Spanish, Creole, and several African languages. On Anguilla, which forms part of the British Leewards, a resort at Shoal Bay West (above) lines the sugar-white beaches that have made the island famous.

The dock of the old boathouse (top) *at English Harbour, Antigua, in the British Leewards; this was a British naval base for almost two centuries. A replica of the pirate ship,* Jolly Roger *(left). Young Antiguan boys on their donkeys* (above).

A traditional steel band plays during a street celebration (right). *The music of these steel band musicians is surprising in its complexity. Not only do they play calypso, but the better bands also perform classical and popular pieces, sounding much like a xylophone orchestra.*

Revellers celebrate during carnival celebrations (below) *on Antigua. The annual event, held from the end of July to the first Tuesday in August, is characterized by calypso music, dancing in the streets (called a 'jump-up' in the Caribbean), masquerades and vibrant parades of elaborately costumed participants.*

Brimstone Hill Fortress (top left) *on St Kitts, in the British Leewards, which was built in the 18th century by the British, was called the Gibraltar of the West Indies. Meticulously restored, the fortress has cannons and a museum displaying both colonial and prehistoric Carib Indian artefacts. It also has a marvellous view of Sint Eustatius.*

An old sugar mill (top right) *on the Rawlins Plantation, St Kitts. Known as Liamuiga, or 'fertile island', in the Carib language, its excellent volcanic soils and moderate climate made the island an important producer of sugar for the British, and it maintains its agricultural role today. An island church* (above) *features colourful Caribbean details.*

The Circus (above), the town centre of the St Kitts capital, Basseterre, features a four-sided clock and is said to be modelled after London's Piccadilly Circus. Although the town has some colonial stone structures remaining, most of the older buildings were destroyed in 1867 in a major fire. The island's Caribelle Batik factory is known for its excellent batik designs (top right), especially skirts and pareos.

Other island art can be found in galleries in Basseterre, which feature paintings and prints of accomplished local artists Rosey Cameron-Smith and Kate Spencer. Although the quiet island has little night life to speak of, around carnival time – which takes place between Christmas and New Year – the ubiquitous masquerades (top left), calypso bands and dancing take to the streets.

Marigot, capital of St Martin, in the French West Indies, is a modern city (opposite top) which enjoys an active tourist trade, and is also one of the Caribbean's top duty-free shopping ports. Many of its traditional West Indian and colonial buildings have been absorbed into new development, especially around the harbour area.

On its more deserted coastlines, the island's natural beauty is dramatic, where rocky shores plunge into clear, turquoise waters (opposite bottom). Boardsailing (top left) is popular at Baie Orientale and Baie de l'Embouchure, on the island's east coast. For locals in Marigot, the market near the docks (above left) offers fresh produce and a selection of seafoods.

The serene harbour (above) at St Barthélemy, or St Barts, is an indication of why the island has been a favourite hideaway for the wealthy for decades.

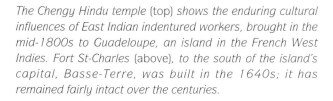

The Chengy Hindu temple (top) *shows the enduring cultural influences of East Indian indentured workers, brought in the mid-1800s to Guadeloupe, an island in the French West Indies. Fort St-Charles* (above), *to the south of the island's capital, Basse-Terre, was built in the 1640s; it has remained fairly intact over the centuries.*

Guadeloupe's Carnaval is a week-long Mardi Gras festival of excess and revelry, held on the days running up to Ash Wednesday, the first day of Lent. In a similar vein to other Caribbean islands that celebrate with their own versions of Carnaval, the highlights are energetic parades of locals dressed in fantastic costumes (above).

Faces of Basse-Terre, a port which focuses on the export of bananas: a young girl of African heritage (top left), and a worker on a banana plantation (above left). Bananas have replaced sugar as the chief crop in modern times, accounting for 60 per cent of all exports, although production was severely affected by the drought of 1994 and the devasta-tion wreaked by Hurricane Debbie shortly thereafter. In Pointe-à-Pitre, an important economic hub in Guadeloupe, the Place de la Victoire (above) has a memorial to French veterans of World War I. A profusion of local flowering plants includes tropical species such as hibiscus, poin-settias, and Flame trees.

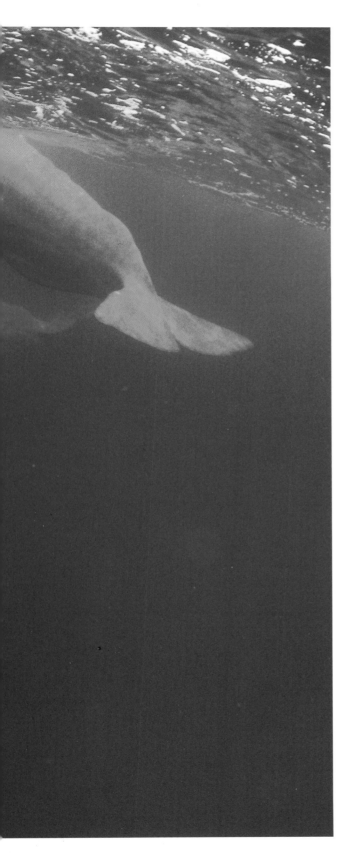

Sperm Whales (Physeter macrocephalus), *one of the world's largest and most majestic whale species* (left), *can be seen off the west coast of Martinique. Reaching a length of 20m (65ft) and nearly 60 tons in weight, Sperm Whales can dive to incredible depths – possibly to below 3200m (10,400ft) – in the search for food. Despite their immense size, they are not aggressive toward people and can be approached by snorkellers.*

The church at Balata (above), *near Martinique's main town, Fort-de-France, was modelled after the Sacré Coeur cathedral in Paris. Indeed, the island is often spoken of as 'a slice of France' in the Caribbean; its natural beauty also lives up to its other popular name, believed to derive from a Carib word meaning 'island of flowers'.*

THE BRITISH WINDWARDS & BARBADOS

Making up the southernmost end of the Windwards chain are former British colonies St Lucia, the nation of St Vincent and the Grenadines, and Grenada, as well as Barbados. Green and fertile, they are the Caribbean's most picturesque islands.

St Lucia, St Vincent and Grenada are rugged volcanic isles that rise steeply from the sea, their interiors covered with verdant rainforest, and they are home to brilliantly plumaged birds and other wildlife. Their volcanic origins are evidenced by cones and crater lakes, although St Vincent is presently the only island whose volcano, La Soufrière, is still active. The first record of any volcanic activity dates back to 1718, but several eruptions have occurred in the intervening years, the worst in 1902, when around 2000 islanders were killed, and in 1979, when spewing ash necessitated the evacuation of 20,000 people from their homes.

The islands, caught between the competing nations of the Spanish, British, Dutch, and French, experienced a chaotic history. Rich volcanic soils made them agriculturally productive too, and their fruits and spices – especially nutmeg, mace and cinnamon – are exported worldwide today.

The Grenadines, a string of small islands and cays sprinkled across an expanse of clear, turquoise-hued water, are quite different from the other Windward islands. They are covered with Coconut Palms and low, salt-tolerant greenery common to coral islands, such as Sea Grape and Buttonwood. As snorkellers and yachtsmen have discovered, the surrounding seas teem with fish, sea turtles and other marine life, while the sea floor is covered with stands of exquisite corals and sea fans.

Barbados is unique – both historically and geographically. Sailing ships had difficulty reaching the island because of its extreme southeasterly location; as a result, it remained out of the mainstream of colonial strife. Though originally discovered by the Portuguese, it was settled by the British and remained a colony, undisturbed by further European colonizers, until 1966. Today, it is the most British of any of the Caribbean isles.

Not of volcanic origin, Barbados is instead a large limestone mound that has gradually risen from the sea as its coralline structures were built upon, and multiplied, over the eons. While it lacks the natural grandeur of the other islands, its rural areas are especially pretty, very much imitating rolling English countryside, complete with neat fences, hedges and a profusion of flowers. Along the coastline, its long, golden-sand beaches are some of the most beautiful to be found anywhere in the Basin. However, the island's large population and well-developed capital city, Bridgetown, place it firmly in the modern world – more so than many other Caribbean islands.

Fishing boats, graceful Coconut Palms and, in the background, one of the twin peaks of the Pitons at quiet Soufrière Bay in St Lucia (left). The island's rain-forest (top) – with Petit Piton and Gros Piton as a backdrop – is home to tall Gommier (gum) and solid Chatagnier trees, with their enormous girths. Deep in the forest, the colourful St Lucia Parrot, endemic to the island, struggles to survive. On the island's west coast, Marigot Bay (above) is a deep, sheltered natural har-bour that has been used since colonial times; today, it is favoured by yachtsmen.

PREVIOUS PAGES
PAGE 136: Picturesque Marigot Bay, St Lucia.
PAGE 137: A local from Grenada.

A group of schoolchildren on St Vincent (above); the largely rural island is one of the few places in the Caribbean where descendants of the original indigenous people still exist. Black Caribs, the result of intermarriage between African slaves and Carib Indians, live in some of the island's villages.

Alluding to its earlier inhabitants, Indian Bay, in the south of St Vincent, offers views across the waters to Young Island (left).

Traditional wooden houses stand along the waterfront on Bay Street (above) *in Kingstown, St Vincent's capital. The centre of the town's bustling market area, the street is lined each morning with stalls selling local produce, for which the island has become known.*

The island's rugged interior mountains (right) *create a lush, dramatic landscape. Thick, forested highland areas and plantations of bananas, arrowroot and Coconut Palms add to the picturesque charm.*

Barbados has the Caribbean's highest population density, with 265,000 residents. The majority live in Bridgetown, the capital city (above). The city's streets and buildings are fairly modern, with a rather metropolitan infrastructure, but tucked in here and there are well-restored colonial buildings. Entertainment for visitors comes in the form of local dance troupes performing to calypso music (opposite) in the island's clubs. In contrast, palm-fringed shores (below) capture the leisurely pace of island life. Barbados is known for its delectable seafood, and an octopus fisherman (right) returns to shore with the morning's catch. The island speciality, however, is a dish made of local Flying Fish.

TRINIDAD AND TOBAGO
& NETHERLANDS ANTILLES

The two-island nation of Trinidad and Tobago – the southernmost of the Caribbean islands – and Aruba, Bonaire and Curaçao of the Netherlands Antilles lie just north of the coast of Venezuela. Saba, Sint Maarten and Sint Eustatius, the remaining Netherlands islands, are located north, in the Leewards, just east of St Croix; lying in the portion of the Caribbean where virtually all ships from Europe, riding the North Equatorial Current, entered the Basin, these small islands were caught up in the several hundred years of struggle between the Spanish, Dutch, French, and English.

Today, Trinidad and Tobago are held to be among the most exotic of the islands in the Caribbean. Known for their natural splendours – the result of a geological time when they formed part of the South American mainland – they have a broader range of ecosystems and plant and animal species than other islands in the region. Trinidad is also the most culturally diverse. Historically, peoples from Africa, India, Europe, China, and Madeira were thrown together on the small island, with each group maintaining its identity over the years, contributing to the exotic mix. Tobago is socially more like the islands of the Leeward chain, with the French, Dutch and British having occupied it at various times; it is believed to have changed hands on at least 29 different occasions during its colonial past. Today, it is enjoyed by tourists for its relaxed pace and beautiful natural setting. The majority of its citizens are of African descent.

The Netherlands Antilles are of two quite different groups. Aruba, Bonaire and Curaçao – the ABCs, as they are called – are very similar. Situated out of the hurricane zone that greatly affects most of the Basin, they are arid and hot, though constantly fanned by the northeastern trade winds. Originally developed by the Spanish and later taken by the English and Dutch, their people are predominantly a mestizo mix of European and native Arawak Indian.

Today, the three islands are known for their upscale resorts, scuba diving and boardsailing. The islands' colonial Dutch charm is strongly evident in their highly colourful buildings and homes.

The other Netherlands islands, in the Leewards – the 'three S's' as they are also known – are small and green, especially Saba, which is the cone of an extinct volcano that rises straight up from the sea and is crowned with rainforest. Tiny Sint Eustatius is of similar volcanic origin, with its long-extinct volcano dominating its landscape. These two islands, away from the mainstream, are quiet and atmospheric and are enjoyed by divers, hikers and bird-watchers. Sint Maarten, occupying one-half of an island with the French St Martin, is hilly and drier; however, it has a convoluted coastline of charming beaches and bays, lined with luxury hotels and resorts.

PREVIOUS PAGES
PAGE 148: *The ruins of early salt raker slave quarters in Bonaire, one of the ABC islands.*
PAGE 149: *Young girls dressed up for the Easter festival in Willemstad, Curaçao.*

Trinidad's Carnaval (above) *is the most festive celebration in the entire Caribbean, said to be rivalled only by Rio's world-famous event; steel bands, costumes and dancing in the streets turn the city of Port of Spain into a gigantic party.*

A local steel band (above right) *plays during Carnaval. Beginning on New Year's Day, groups work into the night in* Mas *(the Trinidadian term for the revelries) camps, creating costumes while bands rehearse around the city to take part in the Band of the Year competition, the* Carnaval *finale.*

A French Baroque-style home (top) *along Queen's Park Savannah in Port of Spain. The most interesting feature of the park, which was formerly a sugar-cane plantation, is a collection of ornate colonial buildings on its west side; one is a reproduction of a Scottish castle, complete with turrets.*

A boardsailor off the coast of Aruba (opposite) takes advantage of the island's location in the path of the trade winds, which blow constantly out of the east-northeast. As it is beyond the hurricane belt, Aruba, together with its sister islands Bonaire and Curaçao, enjoys a hot, dry climate that is kept comfortable by the surrounding sea and a steady breeze.

On Aruba's north coast, wind and waves over the eons have carved a natural rock arch (above) which reaches a length of almost 30m (100ft). The west coast, however, is most noted for its long, dazzling white-sand beaches. Palm Beach (right), perhaps the most developed, has a row of luxury high-rise hotels perched at the edge of its quiet shore.

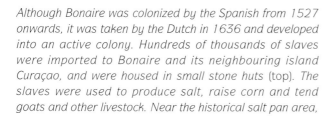

Although Bonaire was colonized by the Spanish from 1527 onwards, it was taken by the Dutch in 1636 and developed into an active colony. Hundreds of thousands of slaves were imported to Bonaire and its neighbouring island Curaçao, and were housed in small stone huts (top). The slaves were used to produce salt, raise corn and tend goats and other livestock. Near the historical salt pan area, which is still used for salt production, the lighthouse at Lacre Point (above left) on Bonaire looms behind the desolate ruins of a slave hut. The island's arid climate supports a variety of drought-tolerant plants, such as acacia, Divi-divi trees and giant cacti (above), which serve as homes for Bonaire's indigenous Yellow-winged Parrot.

The north end of Bonaire is taken up by Washington–Slagbaai National Park, a reserve for the island's plants and animals. Covered with cacti to the edge of the clear sea (top), its bay of Goto Meer, a lagoon, is a feeding area for 15,000 Greater Flamingos. Bonaire is known among divers for its unusual collection of exotic marine creatures. The Longlure Frogfish (above), imitates a colourful sponge;

it wiggles a worm-like lure on its forehead to attract small fish, and when they approach it lunges, swallowing them whole. Among Bonaire's most delightful sea creatures are its Slender Sea Horses (above), which occur in a variety of colours. Sea horses are unusual in that the males incubate the eggs in their belly pouch.

Curaçao's skyline, complete with Dutch gabled and tiled roofs (above), *is one of the most charming in the Caribbean. The island's architecture is a festive, tropical adaptation of 17th-century Dutch style, in the brightest Caribbean hues* (opposite). *The capital, Willemstad, was originally built in the 1700s. Additions were made to its buildings in later years, for example, the galleries which provided shade to counteract the fierce heat, and the tropical colours were later mandated by a governor general who complained that his headaches were caused by the glare of whitewashed buildings.*

At Willemstad's Floating Market (left), *small boats from Venezuela and Colombia arrive each morning and tie up together to sell their fresh fruits, vegetables, seafood, and South American handicrafts.*

HONDURAS, BELIZE, AND THE YUCATAN

Forming the western rim of the Caribbean Basin, the Central American countries of Honduras, Belize and Mexico (along the Yucatán peninsula) share not only the warm Caribbean Sea with the islands of the region, but also their colonial history. Like most of the lands of the New World, the area was developed for agriculture

and other resources, using slave labour. Although originally claimed by the Spanish, the British eventually took control of Belize and parts of Honduras.

One distinct difference that set this area apart from the other lands of the Caribbean, however, was its large population of indigenous people, whose cultural heritage, the Mayan civilization, spanned many centuries. Although many were shipped as slave labour to other islands, and thousands died of disease and maltreatment, the majority of the populations of present-day Mexico and Honduras are descended from the original inhabitants. The Belizean people are predominantly of African descent, although there are numbers of mestizos and Maya as well.

Today, the Caribbean coastal areas of Honduras, Belize and the Yucatán are widely regarded as tourist destinations. Because of the presence of the western hemisphere's longest barrier reef, which runs for 288km (180 miles) along the coasts of the three countries, scuba divers have long discovered the region's remarkable natural resources. In recent years, the Mexican Caribbean, especially around Cancún and Cozumel, has become a world-class tourist region, known not only for its diving, but also for its luxury hotels and the upmarket entertainment it offers.

Honduras and Belize, on the other hand, have begun developing a reputation for their eco-adventure attractions. Diving around the Bay Islands off Honduras and the cays off Belize is well-established. The ocean is known here for its rich marine life and dramatic coral walls.

The two nations also offer visitors a glimpse into one of the world's wondrous ecosystems: the rainforest. Rugged mountain interiors are clothed in humid tropical forest, and the collection of exotic mammals – including majestic big cats like the Jaguar and Ocelot – large reptiles and resplendent birds is world renowned.

Now that the political difficulties of recent years in several neighbouring countries are largely resolved, the region is stable though economically challenged. The effects of Hurricane Mitch on mainland Honduras in 1998 will also be felt for years to come. However, visitors to the three countries are able to enjoy the luxuriant environment, the mysteries of the ancient Mayan culture and gentle, friendly people who are generous with their welcome.

PREVIOUS PAGES
PAGE 162: *A* Garífuna *woman in Trujillo. The* Garífuna, *a mix of African and Carib Indian, were originally deported from St Vincent to the Central American coast by the British.*
PAGE 163: *A Pin Cushion Sea Star sits on a shell-covered sea floor off Roatán, Honduras.*

Colour infuses Caribbean life – whether in scarlet dresses worn to celebrate Black Carib heritage at San Juan's Fiesta Garífuna (above left), *or in bright façades such as this one in the coastal town of La Cieba* (top). *In Honduras, the people are mainly Mayan, like this woman in the capital Tegucigalpa* (above), *or mestizo, a mix of Maya and Spanish.*

Believed by Hondurans to be one of the country's most entertaining cities, La Cieba (top) is the only one on the mainland to celebrate Carnaval in the fashion of the Caribbean islands. The May event, in honour of San Isidro, features food, parades, music, dancing, and beauty contests. Life along the coast has a relaxed pace, as these local card players in the coastal town of El Progresso illustrate (above left). The town is chiefly a transit point for the country's banana crop and for travellers on the way to Tegucigalpa. A mestizo woman browses at a magazine stand in Tegucigalpa (above). The city was first settled in 1578 and today has a population of over a million.

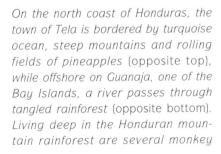

On the north coast of Honduras, the town of Tela is bordered by turquoise ocean, steep mountains and rolling fields of pineapples (opposite top), while offshore on Guanaja, one of the Bay Islands, a river passes through tangled rainforest (opposite bottom). Living deep in the Honduran mountain rainforest are several monkey species, including the Howler, Spider and Capuchin monkeys. The White-face Monkey (above left) is another species of this part of Central America.

Relying on the bounty of the sea, local Bay Islands fishermen set out in a dugout canoe (above). These traditional boats, which are effective in the calm waters around the islands, have been used for many hundreds of years.

Honduran artists have evolved a unique, primitive style of painting, evident in this rendition of a basket-maker (top), by Honduran artist B Nicholas.

Cenotes, once used as sacred wells by the Maya, are still being discovered and explored. They were often the sites of sacrifices and offerings to the gods, and deep jungle pools (opposite top) *have been found to contain amazing collections of artefacts. The wells are part of the region's huge underground cavern system, similar to those explored by divers at Nah Chich* (opposite bottom).

An aerial view of Cozumel (above), *off Mexico's Yucatán coast. A favourite destination for scuba divers, the island's Palancar Reef is one of the Caribbean's most highly re-*garded diving areas. Around the main town of San Miguel, Cozumel has been developed into a major tourist centre, with docks for cruise ships, luxury hotels, restaurants and clubs. Outside the developed area, the island is blessed with long, white-sand beaches and turquoise waters.

The people of the Yucatán (top and bottom) *resisted assim-ilation by the Spanish for centuries, and still manifest Mayan bloodlines, although the Maya disappeared as a culture around 900*AD.

Held by many to be the most ornate of the Mayan temples, Uxmal (above) is believed to have been the central hub for a district that contained many sites. Begun in the sixth century, the complex was rebuilt at least five times.

Chichén Itzá, one and a half hours from Mérida, is a mingling of Mayan and Toltec structures, as the Toltecs built their temples at the original Mayan complex. The Temple of the Grand Mesas (top) *has recently been reconstructed. The Temple of the Warriors* (above left) *stands near the carved Group of the Thousand Columns. Kukulkán, or El Castillo* (above right), *built to strict astronomical guidelines, casts the shadow of a serpent down the north stair at the two equinoxes – 22 March and 22/23 September.*

INDEX